Rust and Functional Programming

Building Expressive, Efficient, and Safe Code with Functional Techniques

Ethan B.Carter

TABLE OF CONTENT

Chapter 3.

Core Rust Concepts

3.1 Error Handling with Option and Result

3.2 Pattern Matching in Depth

3.3 Traits and Generics for Abstraction

3.4 Memory Safety and Performance

Chapter 4

. Foundations of Functional Programming

4.1 Immutability and Pure Functions

4.2 First-Class and Higher-Order Functions

4.3 Functional Data Structures: Lists, Maps, and More

4.4 Understanding Recursion and Tail-Call Optimization

Chapter 5.

Applying Functional Techniques in Rust

Chapter 1.

Introduction to Rust and Functional Programming

Rust is a modern systems programming language designed for safety, performance, and concurrency. Unlike traditional systems languages like C or C++, Rust enforces memory safety through its unique ownership model, preventing common bugs like null pointer dereferencing and data races at compile time. These features make Rust ideal for building reliable and efficient software across domains such as system-level programming, web development, and game engines.

Functional programming, on the other hand, is a paradigm focused on writing programs with pure functions, immutability, and declarative constructs. It emphasizes avoiding shared state and side effects, making code more predictable, easier to test, and maintainable. Functional programming introduces concepts such as higher-order functions, algebraic data types, and pattern matching, which are also prevalent in Rust.

By combining the safety and performance guarantees of Rust with the expressive power of functional programming techniques, developers can write robust, maintainable, and efficient code. Rust's features—like closures, iterators, and pattern matching—align well with functional programming principles, enabling a hybrid approach to programming that leverages the strengths of both paradigms.

This book explores how Rust's design makes it a natural fit for functional programming, offering practical techniques and real-world examples to help developers build expressive, efficient, and safe applications.

1.1 Understanding Rust: Systems Programming with Safety

Rust is a systems programming language designed to empower developers to write low-level, high-performance software without sacrificing safety. Unlike traditional systems languages like C and C++, Rust takes a bold step by enforcing safety guarantees at compile time, reducing the risk of common programming errors such as memory leaks, buffer overflows, and data races.

Key Features of Rust

Ownership and Borrowing:

Rust introduces a unique ownership model that governs how memory is managed. Each value in Rust has a single owner, and the compiler enforces strict rules for borrowing and sharing data. This ensures memory safety without the need for a garbage collector.

Zero-Cost Abstractions:

Rust provides powerful abstractions, like traits and iterators, that are as efficient as hand-written low-level code. This allows developers to write expressive and high-level code without compromising performance.

Concurrency without Data Races:

Rust's ownership model extends to its concurrency model, preventing data races at compile time. Developers can write highly concurrent programs that are both safe and efficient, leveraging tools like threads, async/await, and message-passing.

Memory Safety without Garbage Collection:

Rust avoids runtime garbage collection by relying on compile-time checks to manage memory. This results in predictable performance, making it suitable for resource-constrained environments such as embedded systems or game engines.

Control and Flexibility:

Rust gives developers fine-grained control over system resources, allowing them to write code that interacts directly with hardware or optimizes performance-critical paths.

Applications of Rust

Rust excels in a variety of domains:

Systems Programming: Operating systems, device drivers, and networking tools.

Web Development: Backend services, with frameworks like Actix and Axum.

Embedded Systems: Applications in robotics and IoT.

Game Development: High-performance game engines and simulations.

Rust's focus on safety and performance makes it an excellent choice for developers looking to harness the power of systems programming while avoiding the pitfalls of manual memory management. With its rich feature set and growing ecosystem, Rust is shaping the future of safe and efficient software development.

1.2 Core Principles of Functional Programming

Functional programming is a programming paradigm centered on writing code that is declarative, predictable, and easy to reason about. It emphasizes computation through pure functions, immutability, and higher-level abstractions, enabling developers to build reliable and maintainable software. Below are the core principles of functional programming:

1. Pure Functions

A pure function is a function where:

The output depends only on its input parameters.

It produces no side effects (e.g., modifying global state or performing I/O operations).

Pure functions simplify reasoning about code and make it easier to test and debug. For example:

```rust
Copy code
fn add(a: i32, b: i32) -> i32 {
    a + b
}
```

2. Immutability

In functional programming, data is immutable, meaning once created, it cannot be modified. Instead, transformations produce new data structures. This avoids unintended side effects and makes programs easier to debug. Rust supports immutability by default:

```rust
Copy code
let x = 10; // x is immutable
let y = x + 5; // Produces a new value
```

3. First-Class and Higher-Order Functions

Functions are treated as first-class citizens, meaning they can be assigned to variables, passed as arguments, or returned from other functions. Higher-order functions are functions that take other functions as arguments or return them.

Example with Rust's map function:

rust
Copy code

```
let numbers = vec![1, 2, 3, 4];
let doubled: Vec<i32> = numbers.iter().map(|x| x * 2).collect();
```

4. Declarative Programming

Functional programming emphasizes describing what to do rather than how to do it. This contrasts with imperative programming, which focuses on step-by-step instructions. For example, using iterators in Rust for summing numbers:

```rust
rust
Copy code
let sum: i32 = vec![1, 2, 3].iter().sum();
```

5. Recursion Over Iteration

In functional programming, recursion is often used instead of loops. While Rust supports recursion, it also provides efficient, functional-style iteration through its iterator traits to avoid the performance costs of deep recursion.

6. Algebraic Data Types

Functional programming uses algebraic data types, such as Option and Result in Rust, to represent data in a safe and expressive way. These types enforce exhaustive handling of all possible cases, reducing runtime errors.

rust

Copy code

```
fn divide(a: i32, b: i32) -> Option<i32> {
  if b != 0 {
    Some(a / b)
  } else {
    None
  }
}
```

7. Composition and Modularity

Functional programming promotes building small, reusable functions that can be composed to solve larger problems. This reduces duplication and improves code readability. Rust's function combinators, like and_then and map, help in composing functions elegantly.

8. Lazy Evaluation

Some functional languages support lazy evaluation, where computations are deferred until their results are needed. While Rust is eager by default, it allows for lazy evaluation through iterators and closures.

Functional programming principles enhance code reliability, maintainability, and clarity. Rust's design embraces these principles while balancing them with performance and systems-level control, making it an excellent language for functional programming.

1.3 Why Functional Programming Fits Rust

Rust and functional programming are a natural fit because both prioritize correctness, safety, and simplicity in software design. While Rust is primarily known as a systems programming language, its features and idioms align seamlessly with functional programming principles, offering developers the ability to write expressive and efficient code without compromising safety or performance. Here's why functional programming works so well in Rust:

1. Strong Type System

Rust's strong and expressive type system enables many functional programming constructs. Enums, pattern matching, and generics allow developers to implement functional patterns like algebraic data types and exhaustive case analysis. This reduces runtime errors by enforcing correctness at compile time.

Example with Option type:

```rust
Copy code
fn divide(a: i32, b: i32) -> Option<i32> {
    if b != 0 {
        Some(a / b)
    } else {
        None
    }
}
```

2. Immutability by Default

Rust encourages immutability, a cornerstone of functional programming. Variables in Rust are immutable by default, which makes reasoning about state changes easier and helps prevent unintended side effects.

rust
Copy code
let x = 10; // Immutable by default
let y = x + 5; // Produces a new value

3. Pattern Matching

Rust's pattern matching through the match keyword allows for elegant and concise handling of complex data structures. This aligns with functional programming's emphasis on declarative code and exhaustive handling of all cases.

rust
Copy code
let result = Some(42);

```
match result {
    Some(value) => println!("Value: {}", value),
    None => println!("No value"),
}
```

4. Higher-Order Functions and Iterators

Rust supports higher-order functions, closures, and iterators, making it easy to work with functional abstractions like map, filter, and fold. These constructs allow developers to write concise, declarative, and expressive code.

```rust
Copy code
let numbers = vec![1, 2, 3];
let doubled: Vec<i32> = numbers.iter().map(|x| x * 2).collect();
```

5. Zero-Cost Abstractions

Functional programming can sometimes introduce performance overhead due to abstractions. However,

Rust's zero-cost abstractions ensure that functional constructs like iterators and closures are as efficient as hand-written loops, making functional programming not just expressive but also performant.

6. Ownership and Safety

Rust's ownership model enforces strict memory safety rules, ensuring that functional patterns like immutability and data sharing are handled safely. This prevents issues like data races and null pointer dereferencing that are common in other languages.

7. Built-In Support for Functional Data Types

Rust includes functional data types like Option, Result, and Iterators, which are commonly used in functional programming to handle nullable values, errors, and sequences in a safe and expressive manner.

rust
Copy code
```rust
let sum: Result<i32, &str> = Ok(42).map(|x| x + 10);
```

8. Concurrency with Functional Paradigms

Functional programming naturally aligns with concurrency due to its emphasis on immutability and statelessness. Rust's async/await system and message-passing concurrency models complement this, enabling developers to write safe and efficient concurrent programs.

9. Declarative and Composable Code

Functional programming promotes declarative and composable code. Rust's traits and combinators, such as map, and_then, and unwrap_or, allow developers to build complex logic from smaller, reusable components.

10. A Hybrid Approach

Rust supports a mix of paradigms, allowing developers to combine functional programming with imperative or object-oriented approaches. This flexibility lets developers use functional programming when it simplifies logic while retaining the ability to write low-level, procedural code when performance is critical.

Rust's balance between functional programming principles and low-level control makes it uniquely positioned to provide the best of both worlds. With its emphasis on safety, performance, and expressiveness, Rust is an ideal language for adopting functional programming techniques in real-world applications.

1.4 A Roadmap of the Book

This book, Rust and Functional Programming: Building Expressive, Efficient, and Safe Code with Functional Techniques, is designed to guide readers through the powerful combination of Rust's features and functional programming principles. It provides a structured journey from foundational concepts to advanced techniques, empowering readers to write safe, expressive, and efficient code. Here's an overview of the roadmap:

1. Introduction

We begin by exploring Rust's core philosophy and its alignment with functional programming principles. This section establishes the motivation for combining the two, highlighting the benefits of safety, efficiency, and code maintainability.

2. Fundamentals of Rust

This chapter introduces the essential features of Rust, such as ownership, borrowing, and error handling. By mastering these concepts, readers will understand the foundation that makes Rust a safe and powerful language for systems programming and functional development.

3. Introduction to Functional Programming

Readers are introduced to the core principles of functional programming, including pure functions, immutability, and higher-order functions. These concepts are explained in a way that aligns with Rust's syntax and semantics, laying the groundwork for functional programming in Rust.

4. Functional Techniques in Rust

This section dives deeper into functional programming constructs in Rust, such as closures, iterators, and pattern matching. Readers will learn how to leverage these features to write concise and expressive functional code.

5. Advanced Functional Concepts

For those ready to go beyond the basics, this chapter explores advanced functional programming topics like monads, functors, and combinators. Practical examples show how these concepts can be applied in Rust to handle errors, manage data transformations, and compose functions effectively.

6. Performance Considerations

Functional programming is often associated with abstraction, which can impact performance. This section explains how Rust's zero-cost abstractions allow developers to use functional techniques without sacrificing efficiency. Topics include benchmarking, profiling, and optimizing functional code in Rust.

7. Building Functional Applications

Readers will learn to design and build real-world applications using functional programming in Rust. Topics include state management, handling concurrency, and utilizing Rust's ecosystem to create functional web APIs, data pipelines, and more.

8. Case Studies and Real-World Applications

This chapter showcases practical examples of functional programming in action, including building a concurrent web crawler, a domain-specific language (DSL), and functional processing pipelines. These case studies provide hands-on experience with functional Rust.

Chapter 2.

Getting Started with Rust

Rust is a systems programming language that prioritizes safety, performance, and concurrency. Getting started with Rust involves setting up the development environment, understanding basic syntax, and writing your first program. Below is a concise guide to begin your journey with Rust:

1. Installing Rust

To start, you need to install Rust through the official installer, which sets up the Rust toolchain. This includes the Rust compiler (rustc), the package manager (cargo), and other useful tools. Install it by running:

bash
Copy code
curl --proto '=https' --tlsv1.2 -sSf https://sh.rustup.rs | sh
After installation, verify it with:

bash
Copy code
rustc --version

2. Writing Your First Program

Rust programs start with a main function. Here's a simple program that prints "Hello, world!" to the console:

rust
Copy code
```
fn main() {
    println!("Hello, world!");
}
```
You can compile and run this program using:

bash
Copy code
```
rustc main.rs
./main
```

3. Using Cargo

Cargo is Rust's build system and package manager, which handles compiling, running, and managing dependencies. Start a new project with:

```bash
Copy code
cargo new my_project
cd my_project
cargo run
```

Cargo simplifies the process of building and testing Rust projects.

4. Core Concepts to Learn

As you start coding, focus on key Rust concepts such as:

Ownership and Borrowing: Rust's unique approach to memory management.
Immutability: By default, variables are immutable, encouraging safe and predictable code.
Error Handling: Rust uses Result and Option types for safe error handling.

5. Learning Resources

Rust has a vibrant community and excellent documentation. The official Rust Book is a great place to dive deeper into the language and its features.

Starting with Rust can feel challenging due to its strict compiler, but this strictness is a benefit, as it helps prevent bugs and ensures memory safety. As you get familiar with the syntax and concepts, you'll unlock Rust's power for building safe, concurrent, and efficient systems.

2.1 Installing Rust and Setting Up Your Environment

Setting up Rust on your machine is a straightforward process, and Rust's toolchain is designed to make development efficient and reliable. Here's a step-by-step guide to installing Rust and setting up your development environment:

1. Installing Rust

Rust provides an easy-to-use installer called rustup that manages the installation and updates of Rust and its associated tools. To install Rust, follow these steps:

On Linux/macOS: Open a terminal and run the following command:

```bash
Copy code
curl --proto '=https' --tlsv1.2 -sSf https://sh.rustup.rs | sh
```

On Windows: Download and run the Rust installer from rust-lang.org, or use rustup-init.exe to begin the installation.

Once the installation process is complete, close and reopen your terminal to ensure the system recognizes the new Rust commands.

2. Verifying the Installation

After installation, verify that Rust is installed correctly by running the following command in your terminal:

bash
Copy code
rustc --version
This will display the installed version of the Rust compiler, confirming that Rust is set up properly.

3. Installing Additional Tools

Rust comes with several essential tools bundled via rustup, including:

Rust compiler (rustc): Compiles Rust code.
Cargo: Rust's package manager and build system.
Rustup: Manages Rust versions and updates.

To check if Cargo is installed, run:

```bash
Copy code
cargo --version
```

If both rustc and cargo are available, your installation is complete.

4. Updating Rust

To keep Rust up-to-date, you can run the following command to update your toolchain:

```bash
Copy code
rustup update
```

This ensures you're using the latest stable version of Rust.

5. Setting Up an IDE

While you can write Rust code in any text editor, using an Integrated Development Environment (IDE) or text editor with Rust support will make development much easier. Some recommended IDEs and editors include:

Visual Studio Code (VS Code): Lightweight and highly extensible with the Rust extension.
IntelliJ IDEA with Rust plugin: A feature-rich option for professional developers.
Vim/Emacs: For developers who prefer lightweight, keyboard-centric editors.

These tools provide syntax highlighting, code completion, and integrated debugging for a smooth development experience.

6. Creating a New Rust Project

Once Rust is installed, you can use Cargo to create and manage projects. Create a new Rust project by running:

bash
Copy code

```
cargo new my_project
cd my_project
```

This command generates a new project with a basic directory structure. The src/main.rs file is where your code will go. To build and run the project, simply execute:

```bash
Copy code
cargo run
```

This will compile the project and execute the resulting binary.

7. Configuring Your Environment for Future Projects

Rust also allows you to manage multiple versions of the Rust toolchain (stable, nightly, or specific versions) through rustup. To switch to a different version of Rust, use:

bash

Copy code
rustup default stable

Additionally, you can set up your environment to automatically download dependencies and manage libraries by adding them to the Cargo.toml file in your project directory.

8. Troubleshooting

If you run into issues during installation or setup, the following commands may help:

Check your Rust installation:

bash
Copy code
rustup show

Reinstall Rust:

If things go wrong, you can uninstall and reinstall Rust using:

bash

Copy code

rustup self uninstall

Conclusion

By following these steps, you'll have Rust installed and ready to use, with your development environment configured for maximum efficiency. Once everything is set up, you can begin exploring Rust's powerful features and dive into functional programming and system-level development with ease.

2.2 The Rust Programming Model

Rust's programming model is built around a set of core principles that emphasize memory safety, concurrency, and performance without sacrificing control. At the heart of Rust's design are concepts like ownership, borrowing, and lifetimes, which enable developers to write high-performance, reliable, and concurrent code without relying on a garbage collector. Here's an overview of the Rust programming model:

1. Ownership and Borrowing

One of Rust's most unique and powerful features is its ownership system, which ensures memory safety without the need for a garbage collector. This system is built on three key concepts: ownership, borrowing, and lifetimes.

Ownership: Every value in Rust has a variable that is its "owner." When ownership of a value is transferred from one variable to another, the original variable can no longer access that value. This prevents issues like double freeing memory.

Borrowing: Rust allows variables to temporarily "borrow" references to a value instead of taking ownership of it. There are two types of borrowing:

Immutable borrowing: Multiple immutable references can exist, allowing read-only access to data.

Mutable borrowing: Only one mutable reference can exist at a time, ensuring that no other part of the code can change the data simultaneously, thus preventing data races.

Lifetimes: Lifetimes ensure that references are valid as long as they are in use. Rust uses lifetimes to track the scope of references, preventing dangling pointers and ensuring that references do not outlive the data they point to.

2. Memory Safety Without a Garbage Collector

Rust avoids common pitfalls of manual memory management (e.g., null pointer dereferencing and memory leaks) by enforcing strict compile-time checks for ownership, borrowing, and lifetimes. This design enables fine-grained control over memory while avoiding the runtime cost of a garbage collector. The absence of a garbage collector ensures that memory management overhead is minimal, making Rust an ideal choice for system-level programming.

3. Concurrency Without Data Races

Rust's ownership and borrowing model extends to its handling of concurrency. By ensuring that data is either owned by a single thread or immutably borrowed, Rust guarantees that there can be no data races—one of the most common sources of concurrency bugs in multithreaded programs. Rust's concurrency model allows for safe and efficient parallelism.

Concurrency with Rust: Rust makes it easy to write concurrent programs using its thread model and channels for communication between threads. The ownership system prevents data races at compile time by ensuring that mutable data cannot be shared between threads without proper synchronization.

Async/Await: Rust also supports

asynchronous programming, allowing you to write highly concurrent code without blocking threads. The async and await keywords help you manage asynchronous tasks with minimal overhead, and Rust's borrow checker ensures that references in asynchronous code are handled safely.

4. Type System

Rust has a powerful and expressive type system that supports generic programming and enables safe abstractions. Key features include:

Generics: Rust supports generics for functions, structs, and enums, enabling code that works with many different types while maintaining type safety.

Traits: Traits in Rust define shared behavior and enable polymorphism. You can implement traits for custom types, allowing for flexible and reusable code.

Pattern Matching: Rust has a powerful pattern matching system that allows you to destructure and match against data in a concise and readable manner. This is especially useful when working with enums and algebraic data types (ADTs).

5. Error Handling

Rust handles errors with two main types: Result and Option. These types allow developers to manage errors explicitly and safely, reducing the risk of runtime crashes.

Result: Used for functions that can return an error. It can be either Ok(T) for a successful result or Err(E) for an error.

Option: Used when a value might be absent. It can be either Some(T) for a present value or None for an absent value.

By forcing explicit handling of errors, Rust ensures that many common sources of runtime bugs are avoided at compile time.

6. Immutability by Default

Rust encourages immutability as a default, meaning variables are immutable unless explicitly declared as mutable using the mut keyword. This promotes safer, more predictable code, as data cannot be accidentally modified. However, when mutability is required, Rust allows it with clear constraints, reducing the potential for errors.

7. Functional Programming Support

Rust embraces several concepts from functional programming, making it easy to write functional-style code. These include:

First-class functions: Functions can be assigned to variables, passed as arguments, and returned from other functions.

Closures: Rust supports closures (anonymous functions) that can capture variables from their environment, providing great flexibility in functional programming.

Iterators: Rust provides a rich set of iterator methods (e.g., map, filter, fold) to process collections in a declarative manner.

8. Zero-Cost Abstractions

Rust provides high-level abstractions (such as iterators, traits, and closures) without the runtime overhead typically associated with abstractions. These abstractions are designed to be as efficient as the equivalent low-level code, thanks to the Rust compiler's optimization capabilities. The goal of zero-cost abstractions is to allow developers to write expressive, readable code without sacrificing performance.

Conclusion

The Rust programming model is designed to help developers write safe, efficient, and concurrent software. By enforcing strict rules around ownership, borrowing, and lifetimes, Rust eliminates many common bugs at compile time, ensuring that programs are memory-safe and thread-safe. The model's emphasis on immutability, explicit error handling, and zero-cost abstractions gives developers the power to write high-performance code without sacrificing safety or control. With its blend of low-level capabilities and high-level abstractions, Rust offers a unique and powerful programming model for system-level and concurrent applications.

2.3 Ownership and Borrowing Basics

Rust's ownership and borrowing model is one of its most defining features, ensuring memory safety and preventing common bugs like data races, dangling pointers, and memory leaks. At the heart of this model are three key concepts: ownership, borrowing, and lifetimes. These concepts are designed to manage memory without a garbage collector, allowing Rust to provide memory safety at compile time.

Here's a breakdown of the basics of ownership and borrowing in Rust:

1. Ownership

In Rust, every piece of data has a single owner, which is the variable or object that holds it. Ownership is central to how Rust manages memory, as it determines who is responsible for freeing resources. The rules of ownership are simple:

Each value in Rust is owned by a variable.
There can only be one owner at a time.
When the owner goes out of scope, the value is automatically dropped (deallocated).

This ensures that there are no memory leaks, as the compiler tracks ownership and automatically deallocates resources when the owner goes out of scope.

Example:

rust
Copy code

```
fn main() {
    let x = String::from("Hello, world!"); // x owns the String
    let y = x; // Ownership of the String is moved to y

    // println!("{}", x); // Error: x no longer owns the String, it was moved to y
    println!("{}", y); // This works, as y is the current owner
}
```

In the example above, when ownership of the String is moved from x to y, x can no longer access the value. Rust enforces this ownership rule to prevent issues like double freeing memory.

2. Borrowing

Borrowing allows you to temporarily use a value without taking ownership of it. Rust's borrowing system enables you to share data between different parts of your program safely. There are two types of borrowing: immutable borrowing and mutable borrowing.

Immutable Borrowing: You can have multiple immutable references to a value, but you cannot modify it while it's being borrowed immutably.

Mutable Borrowing: You can have exactly one mutable reference to a value at a time. This ensures that no other part of the code can access or modify the value while it's being changed.

The key rule of borrowing is that you cannot have mutable and immutable references to the same data at the same time. This prevents data races and ensures safety.

Example:

```rust
Copy code
fn main() {
```

```
let s = String::from("Hello, world!");

let s1 = &s; // Immutable borrow
let s2 = &s; // Another immutable borrow

println!("{} and {}", s1, s2); // Both immutable borrows
are valid here

// let s3 = &mut s; // Error: cannot borrow as mutable
because it's already borrowed as immutable
}
```

In this example, s is borrowed twice immutably. Both s1 and s2 are references to s, but no modification is allowed while these references exist. Trying to borrow it mutably while it's already borrowed immutably would result in a compile-time error.

3. Mutable Borrowing

Mutable borrowing allows a function or part of code to modify a value. However, Rust enforces strict rules to avoid race conditions and inconsistent data states. You can only have one mutable reference to a value at a time, ensuring that no other part of your program can access or change the value during the mutation.

Example:

rust
Copy code
```
fn main() {
    let mut s = String::from("Hello");

    let s1 = &mut s; // Mutable borrow
    s1.push_str(", world!"); // We can modify s through s1
    println!("{}", s1);

    // let s2 = &mut s; // Error: cannot borrow `s` as mutable
more than once at a time
}
```

Here, s is mutable, so it can be borrowed mutably. The borrow is valid while s1 is in scope, but you can't have another mutable borrow of s until s1 is no longer in use.

4. Lifetimes

Lifetimes are a way to ensure that references are always valid. In Rust, references must always point to valid data. A reference is said to be valid only as long as the data it points to remains valid. Lifetimes help the compiler track how long references should last to prevent dangling references (i.e., references that point to data that has already been deallocated).

While Rust can often infer lifetimes, you can explicitly annotate them when necessary. The Rust compiler checks lifetimes at compile time to ensure that no reference outlives its data.

Example:

```rust
Copy code
fn main() {
    let s = String::from("Hello, world!");

    let r = &s; // r is a reference to s
```

```
println!("{}", r); // r is valid here, because s is still in
scope
}
```
In this example, the reference r is valid because s exists as long as r does. The compiler ensures that the reference does not outlive the data it points to.

5. The Rule of Ownership, Borrowing, and Lifetimes

Ownership ensures that memory is managed properly and prevents data races and memory leaks by automatically deallocating resources when they go out of scope.

Borrowing allows safe, temporary access to data without taking ownership. Rust ensures that borrowing does not lead to unsafe behavior (such as concurrent mutation of data).

Lifetimes prevent dangling references by ensuring that references are always valid for as long as they are needed.

Conclusion

Rust's ownership and borrowing system enforces memory safety and concurrency safety at compile time, ensuring that data races and memory management errors are caught before runtime. While the concepts of ownership, borrowing, and lifetimes may seem restrictive at first, they provide a foundation that allows developers to write safe and high-performance code. Understanding these principles is essential for becoming proficient in Rust and leveraging its full potential for building reliable and efficient systems.

2.4 Writing Your First Rust Program

Writing your first Rust program is an exciting step into the world of systems programming with a modern language designed for safety and performance. The simplest program you can write is the classic "Hello,

World!" program, which introduces you to basic syntax and the process of compiling and running Rust code.

Here's how to get started with Rust:

1. Setting Up Your Rust Project

Before you write your first program, you need to ensure that Rust is installed. If you haven't already, follow the steps to install Rust using the rustup tool. Once installed, the cargo tool will help manage your project and dependencies.

To create a new Rust project, open a terminal and run the following command:

```bash
Copy code
cargo new hello_world
cd hello_world
```

This command creates a new directory called hello_world with the necessary structure:

Cargo.toml: The configuration file for your project.

src/main.rs: The default Rust source file where your code will reside.

2. Writing the Code

Now, let's write the "Hello, World!" program. Open the src/main.rs file and write the following code:

```rust
Copy code
fn main() {
    println!("Hello, World!");
}
```

Here's what the code does:

fn main(): This defines the main function, which is the entry point of every Rust program. It's where the execution starts.

println!: This is a macro (indicated by the ! symbol) that prints text to the console. In this case, it outputs the string "Hello, World!".

Rust's syntax is simple for such a basic program. The program will print Hello, World! to the console when executed.

3. Compiling and Running Your Program

Now that you've written your code, it's time to compile and run it. Rust uses the cargo tool to manage building and running projects. In the terminal, run:

bash
Copy code
cargo run

This command does two things:

Builds your project (compiles the Rust code into machine code).
Runs the compiled program.
You should see the following output in your terminal:

Copy code

Hello, World!

4. Understanding the Process

Rust programs go through a two-step process before they can be executed:

Compilation: Rust code is first compiled by the Rust compiler (rustc) to produce an executable binary. This compilation ensures that the code adheres to Rust's strict safety and concurrency rules.

Running the Program: After successful compilation, you can execute the binary to see the program's output.

By using cargo, you don't need to manually invoke rustc; Cargo handles this for you, making the process easier and more efficient.

5. Modifying the Program

Once you've written and run the first program, it's helpful to explore how easy it is to modify and experiment with the code. For example, let's modify the program to print your name:

rust
Copy code
```rust
fn main() {
    println!("Hello, [Your Name]!");
}
```

After making the change, run the program again with cargo run, and you should see:

css
Copy code
```css
Hello, [Your Name]!
```

6. Understanding Rust Syntax

At this point, you've learned some essential elements of Rust syntax:

Functions: Defined using the fn keyword, with the function name and a block of code enclosed in curly braces.

Macros: println! is a macro that's called using an exclamation mark !. Rust has several useful macros built into the standard library.

Statements: Rust statements are typically followed by a semicolon (;), signaling the end of a line of code.

7. Next Steps

Congratulations! You've written and run your first Rust program. From here, you can start experimenting with more features of the language, such as:

Variables: Learn about Rust's strict rules around variable mutability and ownership.

Data Types: Explore Rust's primitive types and how to use them.

Control Flow: Experiment with conditionals (if, else) and loops (loop, for, while).

Functions: Dive deeper into defining and using functions, passing arguments, and returning values.

Chapter 3.

Core Rust Concepts

Rust is a systems programming language designed to ensure safety, concurrency, and performance. Understanding its core concepts is crucial to mastering the language and making the most of its features. Below are the fundamental concepts that form the foundation of Rust:

1. Ownership

Ownership is a key concept in Rust that manages memory safety without a garbage collector. In Rust:

Every value has a single owner.
When the owner goes out of scope, the value is automatically deallocated.

Ownership can be transferred (moved) from one variable to another, which ensures that memory is freed once it is no longer in use.

This prevents memory leaks and other common bugs associated with manual memory management.

2. Borrowing

Borrowing allows functions and parts of the program to access data without taking ownership. Rust enforces two types of borrowing:

Immutable borrowing (&T): Multiple parts of the code can read the same data, but no one can modify it while it's borrowed.

Mutable borrowing (&mut T): Only one part of the code can modify the data, ensuring no simultaneous changes.

Rust's borrowing rules prevent data races and ensure memory safety in concurrent contexts.

3. Lifetimes

Lifetimes are a way to ensure that references to data are valid for as long as needed. In Rust, references cannot outlive the data they point to, which prevents "dangling references" (i.e., references to deallocated data). Rust uses lifetimes to track how long references should last and ensures they remain valid throughout the program.

4. Pattern Matching

Pattern matching is a powerful feature in Rust, allowing you to destructure and match against values. Rust's match statement is commonly used with enums and other data types to provide a concise and readable way to handle different possibilities.

Example:

```rust
Copy code
match value {
    Some(x) => println!("Value is {}", x),
    None => println!("No value"),
}
```

5. Traits

Traits define shared behavior that types can implement. Rust's trait system allows you to define interfaces for types, enabling polymorphism. Traits are similar to interfaces in other languages but are more flexible and powerful.

For example:

```rust
Copy code
trait Speak {
    fn speak(&self);
}

struct Dog;
impl Speak for Dog {
    fn speak(&self) {
        println!("Woof!");
    }
}
```

6. Error Handling

Rust uses the Result and Option types to handle errors explicitly, avoiding exceptions. The Result type is used for functions that can return an error, and Option is used when a value may be absent (i.e., Some or None).

Example:

```rust
Copy code
fn divide(x: i32, y: i32) -> Result<i32, String> {
    if y == 0 {
        Err(String::from("Cannot divide by zero"))
    } else {
        Ok(x / y)
    }
}
```

7. Concurrency

Rust's ownership and borrowing rules extend to its concurrency model, ensuring that concurrent code is memory-safe and free of data races. Rust uses the thread module to spawn threads and allows for message passing through channels for communication between threads.

8. Immutability by Default

In Rust, variables are immutable by default, meaning once they are assigned a value, their contents cannot be changed unless explicitly marked as mut. This encourages safer and more predictable code, reducing side effects.

9. Generics

Generics allow for writing flexible and reusable code without sacrificing type safety. In Rust, you can define functions, structs, and enums that can operate on multiple types, and the compiler ensures type correctness at compile time.

Example:

rust
Copy code
```
fn print_value<T>(value: T) {
    println!("{:?}", value);
}
```

Conclusion

These core concepts—ownership, borrowing, lifetimes, pattern matching, traits, error handling, concurrency, immutability, and generics—are fundamental to writing safe and efficient Rust code. By understanding these principles, you can leverage Rust's strengths in systems programming while avoiding common pitfalls like memory errors, data races, and runtime exceptions.

3.1 Error Handling with Option and Result

Error handling is a critical part of writing robust and reliable software. In Rust, error handling is done through two powerful types: Option and Result. These types help to explicitly represent the absence or presence of a value (in the case of Option) and the success or failure of an operation (in the case of Result), making error handling predictable, safe, and easier to manage.

Rust does not rely on exceptions like many other languages, instead opting for an explicit handling approach using these types. This approach eliminates the need for runtime exception handling and gives developers more control over error management at compile time.

1. The Option Type

The Option type is used when a value can either exist or be absent. It is an enum that can have two variants:

Some(T): Contains a value of type T.
None: Represents the absence of a value.

This type is especially useful when a value might not exist, such as looking up a key in a map or parsing user input.

Example:

```rust
Copy code
fn find_name(name: &str) -> Option<String> {
    if name == "Alice" {
        Some(String::from("Alice"))
    } else {
        None
    }
}

fn main() {
    let name = find_name("Alice");

    match name {
        Some(value) => println!("Found name: {}", value),
        None => println!("Name not found"),
    }
```

}

In this example:

find_name returns an Option<String>. If the name matches "Alice", it returns Some(String::from("Alice")), otherwise, it returns None.

The match statement is used to check if the result is Some (a value) or None (no value), ensuring that the absence of a value is handled explicitly.

2. The Result Type

The Result type is used for functions that can either succeed or fail. It is another enum with two variants:

Ok(T): Represents success and contains a value of type T.
Err(E): Represents failure and contains an error of type E.

The Result type is typically used when a function can return a result or an error, such as file I/O, network requests, or dividing numbers.

Example:

rust

Copy code

```rust
fn divide(x: i32, y: i32) -> Result<i32, String> {
    if y == 0 {
        Err(String::from("Cannot divide by zero"))
    } else {
        Ok(x / y)
    }
}

fn main() {
    match divide(10, 2) {
        Ok(result) => println!("Division result: {}", result),
        Err(e) => println!("Error: {}", e),
    }

    match divide(10, 0) {
        Ok(result) => println!("Division result: {}", result),
        Err(e) => println!("Error: {}", e),
    }
}
```

In this example:

The divide function returns a Result<i32, String>. If y is zero, it returns an error (Err), otherwise, it returns the result (Ok).
The match expression checks if the result is Ok or Err, and handles the success and failure cases accordingly.

3. Propagating Errors

In Rust, rather than manually handling every error, you can propagate errors using the ? operator. This operator simplifies error propagation by returning early if the result is an error. This is especially useful when a function calls multiple other functions that can return Result or Option values.

Example:
rust
Copy code
```
fn read_file(filename: &str) -> Result<String, std::io::Error> {
```

```
    let contents = std::fs::read_to_string(filename)?;
    Ok(contents)
}


fn main() {
    match read_file("hello.txt") {
            Ok(contents) => println!("File contents: {}",
contents),
        Err(e) => println!("Error reading file: {}", e),
    }
}
```

In this example:

The read_file function uses ? to propagate any Err value from std::fs::read_to_string. If an error occurs (e.g., the file doesn't exist), the function will return early with the error.

The main function handles the error by matching on the Result.

Using the ? operator streamlines error handling, making code more readable and less verbose.

4. Combining Option and Result

Sometimes, you may need to work with both Option and Result. For instance, a function may fail in two ways: by either failing to find a value or encountering an error while processing the value.

Example:

```rust
Copy code
fn process_data(data: Option<i32>) -> Result<i32, String> {
    match data {
        Some(value) => {
            if value == 0 {

            Err(String::from("Cannot process zero"))
            } else {
                Ok(value * 2)
            }
        }
        None => Err(String::from("No data provided")),
```

```
        }
    }


fn main() {
    match process_data(Some(10)) {
        Ok(result) => println!("Processed data: {}", result),
        Err(e) => println!("Error: {}", e),
    }

    match process_data(None) {
        Ok(result) => println!("Processed data: {}", result),
        Err(e) => println!("Error: {}", e),
    }
}
```

In this example:

process_data returns a Result<i32, String> after checking whether data is Some or None.
If Some, it processes the value, and if None, it returns an error indicating the absence of data.

5. The unwrap and expect Methods

Sometimes you may want to access the value inside an Option or Result directly. Rust provides the unwrap and expect methods, which allow you to do this, but they will panic if the value is None or Err.

unwrap: Unwraps the value or panics if the result is None or Err.
expect: Similar to unwrap, but you can provide a custom error message for the panic.

Example:
rust
Copy code
```
let value = Some(42);
println!("Value: {}", value.unwrap()); // Will panic if None

let result: Result<i32, &str> = Err("Something went wrong");
println!("Result: {}", result.unwrap()); // Will panic if Err
```

While unwrap and expect are useful for quick prototyping, they should generally be avoided in production code because they can cause panics. Instead, handling errors explicitly with match, ?, or other error handling mechanisms is preferred.

Conclusion

Rust's Option and Result types provide powerful, type-safe mechanisms for error handling, ensuring that developers can handle errors at compile time rather than relying on runtime exceptions. The explicit nature of these types reduces the likelihood of overlooked errors and helps build more predictable, safe applications. By mastering these types, you can write robust, reliable, and error-resistant code in Rust.

3.2 Pattern Matching in Depth

Pattern matching is one of Rust's most powerful and expressive features. It allows you to match data against specific patterns and execute different code based on the structure of that data. Rust's pattern matching is extensive, supporting a wide variety of use cases, from matching simple values to destructuring complex data types like tuples, enums, and structs.

In Rust, pattern matching is primarily used with the match statement, but it can also be used in other contexts, such as if let and while let. Pattern matching provides a concise and expressive way to handle various conditions and improve code readability.

1. Basic Pattern Matching with match

The most common use of pattern matching in Rust is the match statement, which allows you to check a value against several patterns and run the corresponding code when a pattern is matched.

Basic Example:

rust

Copy code

```rust
fn main() {
    let number = 3;

    match number {
        1 => println!("One"),
        2 => println!("Two"),
        3 => println!("Three"),
        _ => println!("Other"), // _ is a catch-all pattern
    }
}
```

In this example:

The match statement checks the value of number and prints the corresponding message.

The _ pattern is a catch-all that matches any value not explicitly handled by the other arms.

Patterns in match can be as simple as specific values or more complex structures, like ranges or combinations of types.

2. Destructuring with Pattern Matching

Rust allows you to destructure complex data types, such as tuples, structs, and enums, using pattern matching. This can be incredibly useful for extracting individual components from a data structure.

Matching with Tuples:
rust
Copy code
```
fn main() {
    let point = (3, 5);

    match point {
        (0, 0) => println!("Origin"),
        (x, y) => println!("Point at ({}, {})", x, y),
    }
}
```

Here:

The match statement checks the tuple (x, y) and destructures it into individual components, allowing you to use x and y within the arm.

Matching with Enums:

Rust's enums are commonly used with pattern matching. A match on an enum allows you to handle different variants efficiently.

```rust
Copy code
enum Direction {
    Up,
    Down,
    Left,
    Right,
}

fn move_player(direction: Direction) {
    match direction {
        Direction::Up => println!("Moving up"),
        Direction::Down => println!("Moving down"),
```

```
        Direction::Left => println!("Moving left"),
        Direction::Right => println!("Moving right"),
    }
}
```

In this example:

The match statement matches against the variants of the Direction enum and executes the corresponding action.

3. Pattern Matching with Option and Result

One of the most common use cases for pattern matching in Rust is when dealing with the Option and Result types, which are enums used for handling the presence/absence of a value and success/failure states, respectively.

Option Example:
rust
Copy code
```
fn main() {
    let value: Option<i32> = Some(42);
```

```rust
    match value {
        Some(v) => println!("Found value: {}", v),
        None => println!("No value found"),
    }
}
```

This pattern matching allows you to safely handle cases where a value might or might not exist.

Result Example:

rust
Copy code
```rust
fn process_number(value: Result<i32, &str>) {
    match value {
        Ok(v) => println!("Processing value: {}", v),
        Err(e) => println!("Error: {}", e),
    }
}
```

In both cases, match allows you to destructure and handle both Some/None and Ok/Err values cleanly and safely.

4. Guard Clauses in Pattern Matching

Rust allows you to add guard clauses to patterns, which are additional conditions that must be met for the pattern to match. This is useful when you want to match a value but only under certain conditions.

Example with Guards:
rust
Copy code
```rust
fn check_number(num: i32) {
    match num {
        x if x < 0 => println!("Negative number"),
        x if x == 0 => println!("Zero"),
        x if x > 0 => println!("Positive number"),
        _ => println!("This won't be reached"),
    }
}
```

In this example:

The guard clauses (if x < 0, if x == 0, etc.) are used to add additional conditions that must be true for a match arm to be executed.

5. Multiple Patterns in One Arm

Rust allows you to match multiple patterns in a single arm, separated by a pipe (|). This is useful when different patterns should trigger the same code block.

Example with Multiple Patterns:
rust
Copy code

```
fn describe_number(num: i32) {
    match num {
        0 | 1 => println!("Zero or one"),
        2..=10 => println!("Between two and ten"),
        _ => println!("Other number"),
    }
}
```

Here:

The pattern 0 | 1 matches either 0 or 1.

The pattern 2..=10 matches numbers in the inclusive range from 2 to 10.

This feature helps keep your match arms concise while covering multiple cases.

6. Matching Structs

Rust allows you to destructure structs in pattern matching as well. This is particularly useful when working with custom data types.

Example with Structs:

rust

Copy code

```rust
struct Point {
    x: i32,
    y: i32,
}

fn print_coordinates(point: Point) {
```

```rust
    match point {
        Point { x, y } => println!("Point at ({}, {})", x, y),
    }
}
```

In this example:

The Point { x, y } pattern destructures the Point struct and binds x and y to the values inside the struct.
You can also match specific fields of a struct, enabling fine-grained control over how you handle the data.

7. Matching with References

Rust's pattern matching works with references as well, allowing you to match data without taking ownership or cloning values.

Example with References:
rust
Copy code
```rust
fn print_length(s: &str) {
    match s {
```

```
    "short" => println!("Short string"),
    _ => println!("String length: {}", s.len()),
  }
}
```

In this example:

The string slice &str is matched directly without consuming the data. This allows for efficient pattern matching on borrowed data.

Conclusion

Pattern matching in Rust is a powerful and flexible tool that makes handling various data structures concise and readable. From simple value matching to complex destructuring, pattern matching can help make code more expressive and less error-prone. The ability to match on enums, structs, tuples, and even add guard clauses provides fine-grained control over your logic. By mastering pattern matching, you can take full advantage of Rust's type system and create more robust and maintainable code.

3.3 Traits and Generics for Abstraction

Rust is a systems programming language that provides powerful tools for abstraction, enabling you to write flexible and reusable code. Two of the most important tools for abstraction in Rust are traits and generics. Together, these features allow you to write code that can operate on different types without sacrificing performance or safety.

1. Traits: Defining Behavior

A trait is a collection of methods that can be implemented by types. In Rust, traits allow you to define shared behavior for different types. They act as a kind of interface that types can implement, and are essential for abstraction, enabling polymorphism in a statically-typed language.

Defining and Implementing a Trait

A trait is defined with the trait keyword. Types can then implement the trait, defining the behavior for the methods within the trait.

rust
Copy code
```
// Defining a trait
trait Speak {
    fn speak(&self) -> String;
}

// Implementing the trait for a struct
struct Dog;

impl Speak for Dog {
    fn speak(&self) -> String {
        String::from("Woof!")
    }
}

struct Cat;
```

```
impl Speak for Cat {
    fn speak(&self) -> String {
        String::from("Meow!")
    }
}

fn main() {
    let dog = Dog;
    let cat = Cat;

    println!("{}", dog.speak());  // Outputs: Woof!
    println!("{}", cat.speak());  // Outputs: Meow!
}
```

In this example:

The Speak trait defines a method speak.
Both Dog and Cat implement this trait, providing their own behavior for the speak method.

Trait Bounds

Traits can also be used as bounds for generics. This allows you to write generic functions that only work with types that implement certain traits.

rust
Copy code
```rust
fn print_speak<T: Speak>(animal: T) {
    println!("{}", animal.speak());
}

fn main() {
    let dog = Dog;
    let cat = Cat;

    print_speak(dog); // Outputs: Woof!
    print_speak(cat); // Outputs: Meow!
}
```

Here, the print_speak function is generic over any type T that implements the Speak trait. The trait bound T: Speak ensures that the function will only accept types that have implemented the Speak trait.

2. Generics: Working with Multiple Types

Generics allow you to write code that works with many different types without knowing the exact type at compile time. Rust's generics enable flexible, reusable code while maintaining performance and type safety.

Generic Functions

You can define functions that are generic over one or more types. These functions are written using type parameters, which are placeholders for concrete types that will be specified later.

rust
Copy code
```
// A generic function that works with any type T
fn print_value<T>(value: T) {
    println!("{:?}", value);
}

fn main() {
    print_value(42);        // Works with integers
```

```
    print_value("Hello!");    // Works with strings
}
```

In this example:

print_value is a generic function that accepts any type T. The type T can be any type, and the function will print the value accordingly.

Generic Structs

Rust also allows you to define structs that are generic over types. This is useful for building data structures that can hold different types of values.

```rust
Copy code
// A generic struct
struct Pair<T, U> {
    first: T,
    second: U,
}
```

```
fn main() {
    let integer_pair = Pair { first: 1, second: 2 };
        let string_pair = Pair { first: "Hello", second:
"World" };

            println!("{:?}, {:?}", integer_pair.first,
integer_pair.second); // Outputs: 1, 2
            println!("{:?}, {:?}", string_pair.first,
string_pair.second);   // Outputs: Hello, World
}
```

Here:

The Pair struct is defined to hold two types, T and U. This makes it possible to create pairs of any types, such as integers, strings, or even structs.

3. Combining Traits and Generics

The power of Rust really shines when you combine traits and generics. By combining these features, you can create highly reusable, flexible code that works with different types while ensuring that certain constraints are met.

Generic Functions with Trait Bounds

You can define a generic function with a trait bound, which restricts the types that can be passed to the function. This allows you to apply specific behavior to types that implement certain traits.

rust

Copy code

```rust
// A trait that defines behavior
trait Addable {
    fn add(&self, other: &Self) -> Self;
}

// Implementing the trait for integers
impl Addable for i32 {
    fn add(&self, other: &Self) -> Self {
        self + other
    }
}
```

```
// A generic function that works with types
implementing Addable
fn sum<T: Addable>(a: T, b: T) -> T {
    a.add(&b)
}

fn main() {
    let result = sum(5, 10);
    println!("{}", result); // Outputs: 15
}
```

In this example:

The Addable trait defines a method add.
The sum function is generic over types that implement the Addable trait, ensuring that only types that implement the add method can be used with it.

Generic Structs with Trait Bounds
You can also apply trait bounds to generic structs, ensuring that the types used in the struct adhere to specific traits.

```rust
Copy code
struct Calculator<T: Addable> {
    value: T,
}

impl<T: Addable> Calculator<T> {
    fn new(value: T) -> Self {
        Calculator { value }
    }

    fn add(&self, other: T) -> T {
        self.value.add(&other)
    }
}

fn main() {
    let calc = Calculator::new(5);
    let result = calc.add(10);
    println!("{}", result);  // Outputs: 15
}
```

Here:

The Calculator struct is generic over type T, but with the constraint that T must implement the Addable trait. This ensures that only types that can be added together are allowed.

4. Default Type Parameters and Associated Types

Rust also allows you to set default type parameters for generics and use associated types in traits to simplify complex abstractions.

Default Type Parameters:

You can specify default values for generic types, making them optional for the user of the struct or function.

rust
Copy code
```rust
// Default type parameter for T
struct Wrapper<T = i32> {
    value: T,
```

```rust
}

fn main() {
    let default_wrapper = Wrapper { value: 10 }; // i32 by default
    let float_wrapper = Wrapper::<f64> { value: 10.5 };

    println!("{}", default_wrapper.value); // Outputs: 10
    println!("{}", float_wrapper.value);   // Outputs: 10.5
}
```

Associated Types in Traits:

Associated types allow you to specify a placeholder type within a trait definition, providing flexibility when implementing the trait.

rust
Copy code
```rust
trait Shape {
    type Output;

    fn area(&self) -> Self::Output;
```

```rust
}

struct Circle {
    radius: f64,
}

impl Shape for Circle {
    type Output = f64;

    fn area(&self) -> f64 {
        std::f64::consts::PI * self.radius * self.radius
    }
}

fn main() {
    let circle = Circle { radius: 3.0 };
    println!("Area of circle: {}", circle.area());
}
```

Here:

The Shape trait has an associated type Output, which is defined by the type implementing the trait.

The Circle struct implements the Shape trait, specifying that Output is f64, and the area method returns an f64 value.

Conclusion

Rust's traits and generics provide powerful tools for abstraction, allowing you to write flexible, reusable, and safe code. Traits enable polymorphism by defining shared behavior for types, while generics allow you to write functions and structs that work with a variety of types without losing type safety or performance. By combining traits and generics, you can create highly abstracted yet efficient code that is both expressive and maintainable. These features are essential for writing idiomatic and robust Rust applications.

3.4 Memory Safety and Performance

Rust is known for its unique combination of memory safety and performance. These two features are at the heart of its design, making it a powerful tool for systems programming, where low-level control over memory and high performance are critical. Rust achieves these objectives without compromising safety, offering developers the ability to write safe, efficient, and concurrent code.

In this section, we'll explore how Rust ensures memory safety without a garbage collector and how its design enables performance comparable to languages like C and C++.

1. Memory Safety Without a Garbage Collector

One of the main challenges in systems programming is managing memory safely and efficiently. Traditional languages like C and C++ rely on manual memory management, which is prone to bugs such as memory leaks, dangling pointers, and data races. Rust solves this problem with a system of ownership, borrowing, and lifetimes that guarantees memory safety at compile time.

Ownership and Borrowing

Rust's memory safety model is based on ownership rules that are enforced by the compiler. Every piece of data in Rust has a single owner, and when ownership is transferred, the previous owner can no longer access the data. This prevents issues like double freeing memory or accessing memory after it's been deallocated.

Ownership: A variable owns the data it points to, and the ownership can be transferred or moved.
Borrowing: Rather than transferring ownership, you can borrow data, either immutably or mutably.
Immutable borrowing (&T): Allows multiple references to the data but does not allow modification.
Mutable borrowing (&mut T): Allows one reference to the data with the ability to modify it.

These rules ensure that:

There are no dangling references (references to deallocated memory).
Memory is automatically freed when it is no longer in use, preventing memory leaks.

Example:

rust
Copy code
```
fn main() {
    let s1 = String::from("hello"); // s1 owns the string

    let s2 = &s1; // s2 borrows s1 immutably
    println!("{}", s2); // Can borrow immutably, no issues

    // Ownership is moved when s1 is assigned to s3
    let s3 = s1;
    // println!("{}", s1); // Error: s1 no longer owns the string
}
```

In this example:

s1 owns the string "hello", and it is borrowed by s2 immutably.

After ownership is moved to s3, trying to use s1 results in a compile-time error, preventing the use of data that has already been freed.

Lifetimes

Lifetimes in Rust ensure that references are always valid. Every reference in Rust has a lifetime, which tells the compiler how long a reference can be used before the data it points to is dropped. The Rust compiler uses lifetime annotations to ensure that references never outlive the data they point to.

rust
Copy code

```rust
fn longest<'a>(s1: &'a str, s2: &'a str) -> &'a str {
    if s1.len() > s2.len() {
        s1
    } else {
        s2
```

```
    }
}
```

Here:

The 'a lifetime annotation ensures that both s1 and s2 live at least as long as the returned reference, preventing the function from returning a reference to data that will be dropped.

Rust's ownership and borrowing system, along with lifetimes, provide memory safety guarantees at compile time, without the need for a garbage collector.

2. Performance: Zero-Cost Abstractions

Rust is designed to provide zero-cost abstractions, meaning that higher-level abstractions, such as closures, iterators, and generics, do not incur runtime overhead. This allows Rust to maintain high performance while providing a safe programming model.

No Garbage Collection

Unlike languages that rely on garbage collection (such as Java, Python, or Go), Rust uses manual memory management via ownership. This eliminates the need for a garbage collector that would otherwise introduce unpredictable pauses and overhead during runtime.

Memory is freed when it is no longer needed, based on ownership rules, and does not require a garbage collector to track object lifetimes.

The absence of garbage collection gives Rust predictable performance, which is critical for systems-level programming, where memory and CPU usage must be finely controlled.

Inlining and Optimizations

Rust's compiler, LLVM, performs aggressive optimizations, including inlining of functions and loops. This helps achieve high performance comparable to lower-level languages like C and C++.

rust

Copy code

```
fn add(a: i32, b: i32) -> i32 {
    a + b
}

fn main() {
    let result = add(2, 3);
    println!("{}", result);
}
```

In this example:

The add function can be inlined by the compiler during optimization, meaning the call to add may not incur any overhead.
Inlining reduces the cost of function calls and can optimize the code further by eliminating unnecessary memory allocations.

Efficient Data Structures

Rust provides efficient, low-level data structures like vectors, hashmaps, and hashsets, which can be used for high-performance applications. These data structures are designed to minimize memory allocation and copying, ensuring that code runs efficiently.

```rust
Copy code
fn main() {
    let mut vec = Vec::new();
    vec.push(1);
    vec.push(2);
    vec.push(3);

    for num in vec {
        println!("{}", num);
    }
}
```

In this example:

The vector is dynamically allocated, but it automatically grows as needed. The memory allocation is managed efficiently, and Rust's ownership system ensures there are no unnecessary copies of data.

3. Concurrency and Parallelism

Rust's ownership system also enables safe concurrency, allowing multiple threads to safely share data without the risk of race conditions. Rust ensures that either:

Only one thread has mutable access to the data at any given time (mutable borrowing).
Multiple threads can have immutable access to the data (immutable borrowing).
This model guarantees that concurrent Rust code will not encounter race conditions or undefined behavior, all while being efficient and free of runtime overhead.

Example:
rust
Copy code

```
use std::thread;

fn main() {
    let data = vec![1, 2, 3, 4];
```

```
let handle = thread::spawn(move || {
    println!("{:?}", data); // data is moved into the thread
});

handle.join().unwrap(); // Wait for the thread to finish
}
```

In this example:

The data vector is moved into the new thread, ensuring that the ownership rules are adhered to, and there are no race conditions or data corruption.
Rust's design allows developers to write high-performance concurrent code, where data is safely shared between threads without needing complex synchronization mechanisms.

4. Efficient Memory Management: No Runtime Overhead

Rust's manual memory management is achieved through compile-time checks rather than runtime tracking, ensuring that there is no performance penalty for safety.

The borrow checker enforces memory safety rules at compile time, and there is no need for a garbage collector, which would otherwise add runtime overhead.

Furthermore, Rust's ownership system ensures that memory is allocated and deallocated exactly when needed. The absence of a runtime garbage collector gives developers precise control over memory usage, which is crucial for performance-sensitive applications like game engines, operating systems, and embedded systems.

Conclusion

Rust strikes a balance between memory safety and performance, which is a rare combination in modern programming languages. Its ownership and borrowing system ensures memory safety without needing a garbage collector, while its focus on zero-cost abstractions allows it to achieve performance on par with languages like C and C++. Additionally, Rust's model for safe concurrency ensures that parallel programs can run safely and efficiently, providing further performance gains.

By combining memory safety with high performance, Rust offers a unique solution for systems programming that allows developers to write efficient and reliable code without sacrificing safety or control.

Chapter 4

. Foundations of Functional Programming

Functional programming is a programming paradigm that emphasizes writing programs by composing pure functions and leveraging immutable data structures. Unlike imperative programming, which focuses on modifying state and sequences of commands, functional programming centers around the mathematical concept of functions and their application.

Key Concepts of Functional Programming

Pure Functions

A function is considered pure if it always produces the same output for the same input and has no side effects.

Example:
rust
Copy code

```
fn square(x: i32) -> i32 {
```

```
    x * x
}
```

Immutability

In functional programming, data is immutable by default, meaning once created, it cannot be changed. Rust embraces immutability, encouraging safer and more predictable code.

Higher-Order Functions

Functions can accept other functions as arguments or return them as results, enabling code reusability and abstraction.

Example:

```rust
Copy code
fn apply_function<F>(x: i32, f: F) -> i32
where
    F: Fn(i32) -> i32,
```

```
{
    f(x)
}

fn main() {
    let result = apply_function(5, |n| n * 2);
    println!("{}", result); // Outputs: 10
}
```

Recursion

Functional programming often replaces loops with recursion for iteration. Rust supports recursion but requires careful handling to avoid stack overflows.

First-Class and Anonymous Functions

Functions are treated as first-class citizens and can be assigned to variables, passed as arguments, or returned from other functions. Rust's closures allow for compact, anonymous functions.

Composition and Modularity

Functional programming promotes breaking down problems into smaller, reusable functions that can be composed together to form solutions.

Advantages of Functional Programming in Rust

Safety: Immutability and pure functions reduce bugs and make programs easier to reason about.

Concurrency: Immutable data eliminates race conditions, enabling safer parallel execution.

Expressiveness: Functional constructs like iterators and closures make code concise and readable.

By combining functional programming principles with Rust's emphasis on memory safety and performance, developers can build robust, efficient, and maintainable software systems.

4.1 Immutability and Pure Functions

Immutability and pure functions are two foundational principles of functional programming that promote code safety, readability, and predictability. Rust embraces these concepts, allowing developers to write reliable and efficient code.

1. Immutability

Immutability means that once a value is assigned, it cannot be changed. Immutable data ensures that the state of a program does not change unexpectedly, reducing bugs caused by unintended side effects.

In Rust, variables are immutable by default. To make a variable mutable, you explicitly declare it with the mut keyword.

Example: Immutable Variables in Rust

rust
Copy code
```
fn main() {
    let x = 10; // Immutable variable
```

```
// x = 20; // Error: cannot assign twice to immutable
variable
    println!("x is {}", x);
}
```

Advantages of Immutability

Thread Safety: Immutable data can be shared across threads without synchronization.

Predictability: Values do not change unexpectedly, making code easier to understand and debug.

Simplified Reasoning: Immutable data ensures that functions behave consistently, as their inputs cannot be modified externally.

Rust allows for efficient handling of immutability through ownership and borrowing, enabling developers to work with data immutably without unnecessary copying.

2. Pure Functions

A pure function is a function that:

Always produces the same output for the same input.

Has no side effects (does not modify external state or rely on external state).
Pure functions are predictable and easier to test because their behavior is isolated from the rest of the program.

Example: Pure Function in Rust

rust
Copy code
```rust
fn add(a: i32, b: i32) -> i32 {
    a + b // No side effects, consistent output
}

fn main() {
    let result = add(3, 4);
    println!("Result is {}", result); // Outputs: Result is 7
}
```

Impure Function Example

An impure function, in contrast, modifies external state or depends on it.

```rust
Copy code
let mut counter = 0;

fn increment() {
    counter += 1; // Modifies external state
}
```

Impure functions can lead to unpredictable behavior and make debugging more challenging.

Benefits of Immutability and Pure Functions

Concurrency: Immutability eliminates race conditions, enabling safe multi-threaded programs.
Debugging and Testing: Pure functions are easy to test because their output depends solely on their input.

Reusability: Pure functions and immutable data encourage modular code that can be reused in different contexts.

Ease of Reasoning: Developers can reason about code more easily when it is free of side effects and unexpected state changes.

Immutability in Rust's Context

While immutability is the default in Rust, the language balances immutability with performance through techniques like interior mutability (using types like RefCell and Mutex) for cases where controlled mutation is necessary.

Conclusion

Immutability and pure functions are key to writing safe, predictable, and maintainable code. Rust's emphasis on immutability by default and its functional programming features, like closures and higher-order functions, allow developers to leverage these principles while maintaining high performance. By combining these concepts with Rust's ownership model, developers can write robust, concurrent, and efficient programs.

4.2 First-Class and Higher-Order Functions

Functional programming treats functions as first-class citizens, meaning they can be passed around and manipulated like any other value. This leads to powerful programming constructs, such as higher-order functions, which take other functions as arguments or return them as results. Rust supports both concepts, enabling expressive and modular code.

1. First-Class Functions

A function is considered first-class when it can:

Be assigned to variables.
Be passed as an argument to other functions.
Be returned from other functions.

In Rust, functions and closures (anonymous functions) are treated as first-class values, allowing flexible program design.

Example: Assigning Functions to Variables

rust
Copy code
```rust
fn multiply_by_two(x: i32) -> i32 {
    x * 2
}


fn main() {
    let func = multiply_by_two; // Assigning a function to a variable
    println!("{}", func(5));   // Outputs: 10
}
```

Example: Using Closures

rust
Copy code
```rust
fn main() {
```

```rust
    let add = |x: i32, y: i32| x + y; // Closure
    println!("{}", add(3, 4));     // Outputs: 7
}
```

2. Higher-Order Functions

A higher-order function is a function that either:

Accepts other functions as parameters.
Returns a function as its result.
Rust supports higher-order functions, which are commonly used for tasks like iteration, transformation, and composition.

Example: Passing Functions as Arguments

```rust
rust
Copy code
fn apply<F>(x: i32, func: F) -> i32
where
    F: Fn(i32) -> i32,
{
    func(x)
```

```rust
}

fn square(x: i32) -> i32 {
    x * x
}

fn main() {
    let result = apply(4, square); // Pass function as argument
    println!("{}", result);     // Outputs: 16
}
```

Here, apply is a higher-order function that accepts a function func as a parameter and applies it to the input x.

Example: Returning Functions

.

rust
Copy code
```rust
fn create_multiplier(factor: i32) -> impl Fn(i32) -> i32 {
    move |x| x * factor
}
```

```rust
fn main() {
    let double = create_multiplier(2); // Returns a closure
    println!("{}", double(5));      // Outputs: 10
}
```

In this example, create_multiplier returns a closure that multiplies its input by a specified factor.

Common Higher-Order Functions in Rust

Rust's standard library provides many higher-order functions, particularly for working with iterators and collections:

map: Transforms each element in a collection using a function.

rust
Copy code
```rust
fn main() {
    let nums = vec![1, 2, 3, 4];
    let squares: Vec<_> = nums.iter().map(|x| x * x).collect();
```

```rust
    println!("{:?}", squares); // Outputs: [1, 4, 9, 16]
}
```

filter: Filters elements based on a predicate.

rust
Copy code
```rust
fn main() {
    let nums = vec![1, 2, 3, 4];
    let evens: Vec<_> = nums.iter().filter(|&&x| x % 2 == 0).collect();
    println!("{:?}", evens); // Outputs: [2, 4]
}
```

fold: Accumulates values using an initial value and a closure.

rust
Copy code
```rust
fn main() {
    let nums = vec![1, 2, 3, 4];
    let sum = nums.iter().fold(0, |acc, &x| acc + x);
    println!("{}", sum); // Outputs: 10
```

}

Advantages of First-Class and

Higher-Order Functions

Code Reusability: Abstract operations like filtering, mapping, and reducing can be encapsulated and reused.
Readability: Expressive constructs lead to concise and easy-to-understand code.
Modularity: Functions can be composed and combined to solve complex problems step by step.

Conclusion

Rust's support for first-class and higher-order functions allows developers to write expressive, flexible, and modular code. By treating functions as values and leveraging higher-order functions, developers can build abstractions, simplify complex operations, and write more reusable code. These capabilities make Rust well-suited for functional programming while retaining its focus on safety and performance.

4.3 Functional Data Structures: Lists, Maps, and More

Functional data structures are designed to be immutable and efficient, aligning with the principles of functional programming. These structures allow the creation of new versions of the data without modifying the original, enabling safe, predictable, and concurrent programming. Rust, though not a purely functional language, provides powerful tools and libraries to work with such data structures.

1. Immutable Lists

Immutable lists are a cornerstone of functional programming. They allow efficient operations like prepending, appending, and traversal without altering the original structure.

Example: Using Vec in Rust

Rust's standard library provides Vec, a growable list. While Vec itself is mutable, you can create immutable versions by avoiding mutation:

rust
Copy code
```
fn main() {
    let list = vec![1, 2, 3, 4];
     let new_list = [&list[..], &[5]].concat(); // Create a new list
    println!("{:?}", new_list); // Outputs: [1, 2, 3, 4, 5]
}
```

Persistent Lists

For fully functional lists, third-party libraries like im provide persistent lists, where modifications result in new versions without copying the entire structure.

rust
Copy code
```
use im::Vector;
```

```rust
fn main() {
    let list = Vector::new() + 1 + 2 + 3;
    let updated_list = list.push_back(4); // Creates a new
list
    println!("{:?}", list);      // Outputs: [1, 2, 3]
    println!("{:?}", updated_list); // Outputs: [1, 2, 3, 4]
}
```

2. Maps (Dictionaries)

Immutable maps (key-value stores) are widely used in functional programming for efficient lookups, updates, and deletions.

Example: Using HashMap in Rust

The standard HashMap in Rust is mutable by default, but you can use functional techniques to create new maps without mutating the original.

rust
Copy code
use std::collections::HashMap;

```
fn main() {
    let mut map = HashMap::new();
    map.insert("key1", "value1");
    map.insert("key2", "value2");

    let new_map: HashMap<_, _> = map.iter().map(|(k, v)|
(*k, *v)).collect(); //
```

Immutable clone

```
    println!("{:?}", new_map); // Outputs: {"key1": "value1",
"key2": "value2"}
}
```

Persistent Maps

Libraries like im also provide persistent maps, enabling immutable updates:

rust
Copy code
use im::HashMap;

```rust
fn main() {
    let map = HashMap::new().update("key1", "value1");
    let updated_map = map.update("key2", "value2");
    println!("{:?}", map);      // Outputs: {"key1": "value1"}
        println!("{:?}", updated_map); // Outputs: {"key1":
"value1", "key2": "value2"}
}
```

3. Sets

Immutable sets ensure no duplicate elements and support efficient membership checks. Rust's HashSet can be used in an immutable context, or you can use libraries like im for persistent sets.

rust
Copy code
```rust
use im::HashSet;

fn main() {
    let set = HashSet::new() + 1 + 2 + 3;
    let new_set = set + 4;
```

```rust
    println!("{:?}", set);    // Outputs: {1, 2, 3}
    println!("{:?}", new_set); // Outputs: {1, 2, 3, 4}
}
```

4. Trees

Trees are fundamental for functional programming, particularly for tasks like expression parsing or hierarchical data storage. Rust supports recursive data structures for tree implementation.

Example: Binary Tree in Rust

rust
Copy code
```rust
#[derive(Debug)]
enum Tree {
    Empty,
    Node(i32, Box<Tree>, Box<Tree>),
}

fn main() {
    use Tree::*;
```

```rust
    let tree = Node(1, Box::new(Node(2, Box::new(Empty),
Box::new(Empty))), Box::new(Empty));
    println!("{:?}", tree);
}
```

For persistent trees, external libraries like im provide balanced tree implementations.

5. Functional Iterators

Iterators are not a data structure per se, but they allow functional-style transformations of data like mapping, filtering, and folding. Rust's iterator API is heavily inspired by functional programming.

Example: Functional Transformations

```rust
Copy code
fn main() {
    let nums = vec![1, 2, 3, 4];
    let squares: Vec<_> = nums.iter().map(|x| x * x).collect();
```

```rust
    let even_squares: Vec<_> = squares.into_iter().filter(|x|
x % 2 == 0).collect();
    println!("{:?}", even_squares); // Outputs: [4, 16]
}
```

Advantages of Functional Data Structures

Immutability: Prevents unintended state changes, ensuring thread safety and easier debugging.

Persistence: Changes result in new versions, preserving the original structure without full duplication.

Concurrency: Immutable data structures eliminate race conditions, simplifying parallel programming.

Modularity: Easier to reason about and combine in functional-style programming.

Conclusion

Rust's ecosystem, with its native collections and third-party libraries like im, allows developers to work with functional data structures effectively. Whether using persistent lists, maps, or trees, these tools align well with Rust's focus on safety and performance, making it an excellent choice for functional programming.

4.4 Understanding Recursion and Tail-Call Optimization

Recursion is a fundamental concept in functional programming, where a function calls itself to solve smaller instances of the same problem. It is especially useful for tasks like traversing data structures, performing repetitive computations, and implementing algorithms elegantly. However, recursion can be inefficient if not optimized, as it often requires additional stack frames. This is where tail-call optimization (TCO) comes into play.

1. What is Recursion?

Recursion is a technique where a function calls itself to break down a problem into smaller, more manageable sub-problems.

Components of a Recursive Function

Base Case: The condition that terminates the recursion to avoid infinite loops.
Recursive Case: The logic that moves the function closer to the base case.

Example: Factorial Function (Recursive)
rust
Copy code
```rust
fn factorial(n: u32) -> u32 {
    if n == 0 {
        1 // Base case
    } else {
        n * factorial(n - 1) // Recursive case
    }
}
```

```
fn main() {
    println!("{}", factorial(5)); // Outputs: 120
}
```

2. Challenges with Recursion in Rust

Rust does not currently implement automatic tail-call optimization due to its low-level control over stack memory and the potential for introducing performance overhead. As a result:

Recursive functions can cause stack overflow for large inputs.
Developers need to carefully manage recursion depth.

3. What is Tail-Call Optimization (TCO)?

Tail-call optimization is a compiler optimization technique that eliminates the need for additional stack frames when a function call is in the tail position. A tail position means the function call is the last operation performed before returning a result.

Why TCO Matters

Prevents Stack Overflow: By reusing the current function's stack frame, the program avoids exceeding stack limits.

Improves Performance: Reduces the overhead of creating and destroying stack frames.

Example of a Tail Call

```rust
Copy code
fn factorial_tail(n: u32, acc: u32) -> u32 {
    if n == 0 {
        acc // Tail position
    } else {
        factorial_tail(n - 1, acc * n) // Tail call
    }
}

fn main() {
    println!("{}", factorial_tail(5, 1)); // Outputs: 120
}
```

In this example, the recursive call to factorial_tail is the last operation, making it a tail call. However, Rust does not optimize this automatically.

4. Simulating Tail-Call Optimization in Rust

To avoid stack overflow in recursive functions, Rust developers often use iteration or manual stack management to simulate TCO.

Using Iteration Instead of Recursion

rust
Copy code
```rust
fn factorial_iterative(n: u32) -> u32 {
    let mut acc = 1;
    for i in 1..=n {
        acc *= i;
    }
    acc
}
```

```rust
fn main() {
    println!("{}", factorial_iterative(5)); // Outputs: 120
}
```

Using a Stack to Simulate Recursion

rust

Copy code

```rust
fn factorial_stack(n: u32) -> u32 {
    let mut stack = vec![];
    let mut result = 1;
    for i in 1..=n {
        stack.push(i);
    }
    while let Some(val) = stack.pop() {
        result *= val;
    }
    result
}

fn main() {
    println!("{}", factorial_stack(5)); // Outputs: 120
}
```

5. When to Use Recursion in Rust

While recursion can be elegant, it is best used:

For problems with a small recursion depth.
When working with divide-and-conquer algorithms (e.g., quicksort, mergesort).
In scenarios where clarity and expressiveness are more important than raw performance.
For tasks with a large recursion depth, prefer iteration or use a crate like recursion to safely handle recursion.

6. Alternatives for Optimized Recursion

Crates and Libraries: Libraries like im offer persistent data structures that can simplify recursion.
Memoization: Cache intermediate results to avoid redundant computations.

rust
Copy code

```rust
use std::collections::HashMap;

fn fib_memo(n: u32, memo: &mut HashMap<u32, u32>)
-> u32 {
  if n <= 1 {
    return n;
  }
  if let Some(&result) = memo.get(&n) {
    return result;
  }
   let result = fib_memo(n - 1, memo) + fib_memo(n - 2,
memo);
  memo.insert(n, result);
  result
}

fn main() {
  let mut memo = HashMap::new();
  println!("{}", fib_memo(10, &mut memo)); // Outputs: 55
}
```

Conclusion

Recursion is a powerful tool for solving complex problems elegantly, but it has its limitations in Rust due to the lack of automatic tail-call optimization. By understanding recursion's challenges and alternatives, such as iteration, memoization, and manual stack management, Rust developers can strike a balance between clarity and performance. For large-scale recursive problems, iterative approaches or external libraries are often the best solutions.

Chapter 5.

Applying Functional Techniques in Rust

Rust, while not a purely functional language, incorporates many functional programming features that enable developers to write expressive, modular, and safe code. By leveraging these features, Rust developers can adopt functional paradigms to enhance code clarity and robustness without sacrificing performance.

1. Immutability

Immutability is a key concept in functional programming, where data cannot be modified after it is created. Rust enforces immutability by default:

rust

Copy code

```rust
fn main() {
    let x = 10; // Immutable by default
    // x = 20; // This would cause a compile-time error
}
```

Immutability reduces unintended side effects and improves code safety, especially in concurrent applications.

2. Higher-Order Functions and Closures

Rust allows passing functions or closures as arguments, enabling reusable and composable code.

```rust
Copy code
fn apply<F>(x: i32, func: F) -> i32
where
    F: Fn(i32) -> i32,
{
    func(x)
}
```

```rust
fn main() {
    let square = |x| x * x;
    println!("{}", apply(4, square)); // Outputs: 16
}
```

3. Iterators and Lazy Evaluation

Functional programming encourages processing collections using iterators, which Rust implements efficiently.

rust
Copy code
```rust
fn main() {
    let nums = vec![1, 2, 3, 4];
    let squares: Vec<_> = nums.iter().map(|x| x * x).collect();
    println!("{:?}", squares); // Outputs: [1, 4, 9, 16]
}
```

Iterators enable lazy evaluation, meaning computations are only performed when needed, optimizing performance.

4. Algebraic Data Types

Rust's enum and Option types provide a robust way to model data and handle edge cases, such as nullability and errors, in a functional style.

rust
Copy code
```rust
fn divide(a: i32, b: i32) -> Option<i32> {
    if b == 0 {
        None
    } else {
        Some(a / b)
    }
}
```

5. Pattern Matching

Rust's powerful pattern matching with match and if let simplifies complex control flows in a functional manner:

rust
Copy code

```rust
fn main() {
    let result = Some(42);
    match result {
        Some(value) => println!("Value: {}", value),
        None => println!("No value"),
    }
}
```

6. Composition and Chaining

Rust's iterator methods and functional traits enable chaining operations for clean, concise transformations:

rust
Copy code
```rust
fn main() {
    let nums = vec![1, 2, 3, 4];
    let result: Vec<_> = nums
        .iter()
        .map(|x| x * 2)
        .filter(|x| x > 4)
        .collect();
    println!("{:?}", result); // Outputs: [6, 8]
```

}

Conclusion

By adopting functional techniques like immutability, higher-order functions, pattern matching, and lazy evaluation, Rust developers can write safer, more expressive code. These features, combined with Rust's performance and safety guarantees, make it an excellent choice for functional-style programming.

5.1 Closures and Their Power

Closures in Rust are anonymous functions that can capture variables from their surrounding scope. They provide a concise and flexible way to define behavior, making them a powerful tool for writing modular and expressive code.

1. What Are Closures?

A closure is a function-like construct that can capture variables from its environment. Unlike regular functions, closures are defined inline and do not require a name.

Basic Syntax
rust
Copy code
```rust
let add = |a: i32, b: i32| a + b; // A closure that adds two numbers
println!("{}", add(3, 4)); // Outputs: 7
```

2. Capturing the Environment

Closures can access and "capture" variables from their surrounding context, which makes them different from regular functions.

Example: Capturing Variables

rust
Copy code

```rust
fn main() {
    let multiplier = 2;
    let multiply = |x: i32| x * multiplier; // Captures
`multiplier` from the environment
    println!("{}", multiply(5)); // Outputs: 10
}
```

Rust determines how a closure captures variables in one of three ways:

By Reference (&T)
By Mutable Reference (&mut T)
By Value (T)

The capture method depends on how the closure is used.

3. Type Inference and Flexibility

Rust allows closures to omit type annotations in most cases, as the compiler can infer types.

rust
Copy code

```rust
let square = |x| x * x;
println!("{}", square(4)); // Outputs: 16
```

For more complex closures or when needed, you can explicitly specify types:

rust

Copy code

```rust
let square: fn(i32) -> i32 = |x: i32| x * x;
```

4. Using Closures with Iterators

One of the most common use cases for closures in Rust is with iterators, enabling functional-style transformations and filters.

rust

Copy code

```rust
fn main() {
    let nums = vec![1, 2, 3, 4];
    let squares: Vec<_> = nums.iter().map(|x| x * x).collect();
    println!("{:?}", squares); // Outputs: [1, 4, 9, 16]
}
```

5. Closures and Traits

Closures in Rust implement one or more of the following traits:

Fn: For closures that don't mutate the environment.
FnMut: For closures that mutate the environment.
FnOnce: For closures that consume the environment.

Example: Closure Traits

rust
Copy code
```rust
fn call_closure<F>(func: F)
where
    F: Fn(i32) -> i32,
{
    println!("{}", func(5));
}

fn main() {
    let add_one = |x| x + 1;
    call_closure(add_one); // Outputs: 6
```

}

6. Closures and Lifetimes

Closures that borrow variables from the environment are subject to Rust's ownership and lifetime rules. This ensures safe access and prevents dangling references.

Example: Borrowing Variables
rust
Copy code
```rust
fn main() {
    let mut count = 0;
    let mut increment = || count += 1; // Mutably borrows `count`
    increment();
    increment();
    println!("{}", count); // Outputs: 2
}
```

7. Storing Closures

Closures can be stored in variables, passed as arguments, or returned from functions. However, to store closures in a struct or dynamically, you often use trait objects like Box<dyn Fn()>.

Example: Returning a Closure
rust
Copy code
```
fn make_adder(x: i32) -> impl Fn(i32) -> i32 {
    move |y| x + y // Captures `x` by value
}

fn main() {
    let add_five = make_adder(5);
    println!("{}", add_five(3)); // Outputs: 8
}
```

8. Performance Considerations

Closures in Rust are highly optimized and often result in zero-cost abstractions. However, capturing variables by value or using trait objects may involve additional memory overhead.

Conclusion

Closures in Rust offer a powerful way to write concise and flexible code. By capturing variables from their environment, working seamlessly with iterators, and adhering to Rust's strict ownership rules, closures strike a balance between expressiveness and safety. They empower developers to write modular, functional-style code while maintaining Rust's performance guarantees.

5.2 The Iterator Trait and Functional Composition

Rust's Iterator trait is a cornerstone of its functional programming capabilities. It provides a way to process collections lazily, enabling clean, modular, and efficient code. Combined with functional composition, the iterator pattern helps developers write expressive code that avoids side effects and focuses on data transformations.

1. The Iterator Trait

The Iterator trait is implemented by types that can produce a sequence of values, one at a time. It defines the core method:

rust
Copy code
```
trait Iterator {
    type Item;
    fn next(&mut self) -> Option<Self::Item>;
}
```

Item: The type of value produced by the iterator.

next: Advances the iterator and returns the next value or None if the sequence is finished.

Basic Example

rust

Copy code

```rust
fn main() {
    let nums = vec![1, 2, 3];
    let mut iter = nums.iter(); // Creates an iterator

    while let Some(value) = iter.next() {
        println!("{}", value); // Outputs: 1, 2, 3
    }
}
```

2. Functional Composition with Iterators

Functional composition involves chaining multiple operations to transform data. Rust's iterators support this with methods like map, filter, and fold.

Common Iterator Methods

map: Transforms each element.

rust

Copy code

```rust
let nums = vec![1, 2, 3];
let squares: Vec<_> = nums.iter().map(|x| x * x).collect();
println!("{:?}", squares); // Outputs: [1, 4, 9]
```

filter: Retains elements that satisfy a condition.

rust
Copy code
```rust
let nums = vec![1, 2, 3, 4];
let evens: Vec<_> = nums.iter().filter(|&&x| x % 2 == 0).collect();
println!("{:?}", evens); // Outputs: [2, 4]
```

fold: Reduces elements to a single value.

rust
Copy code
```rust
let nums = vec![1, 2, 3];
let sum = nums.iter().fold(0, |acc, &x| acc + x);
println!("{}", sum); // Outputs: 6
```

take and skip: Limit or skip elements.

rust

Copy code

```rust
let nums = vec![1, 2, 3, 4, 5];
let subset: Vec<_> = nums.iter().skip(1).take(3).collect();
println!("{:?}", subset); // Outputs: [2, 3, 4]
```

3. Lazy Evaluation

Rust iterators are lazy, meaning operations like map or filter only execute when a terminal method (like collect or fold) is called. This avoids unnecessary computations and improves performance.

Example of Laziness

rust

Copy code

```rust
fn main() {
    let nums = vec![1, 2, 3, 4];
    let iter = nums.iter().map(|x| x * x); // Nothing is executed yet

    for square in iter {
        println!("{}", square); // Computations happen here
```

```
    }
}
```

4. Custom Iterators

Developers can implement their own iterators by defining the next method.

Example: Custom Iterator

```rust
Copy code
struct Counter {
    count: u32,
}

impl Counter {
    fn new() -> Self {
        Counter { count: 0 }
    }
}

impl Iterator for Counter {
```

```rust
    type Item = u32;

    fn next(&mut self) -> Option<Self::Item> {
        self.count += 1;
        if self.count <= 5 {
            Some(self.count)
        } else {
            None
        }
    }
}

fn main() {
    let mut counter = Counter::new();
    while let Some(value) = counter.next() {
        println!("{}", value); // Outputs: 1, 2, 3, 4, 5
    }
}
```

5. Combining Iterators with Functional Composition

Chaining multiple iterator methods results in concise and declarative code.

Example: Transforming and Filtering Data

rust

Copy code

```rust
fn main() {
    let nums = vec![1, 2, 3, 4, 5];
    let result: Vec<_> = nums
        .iter()
        .map(|x| x * 2)
        .filter(|x| x > 5)
        .collect();
    println!("{:?}", result); // Outputs: [6, 8, 10]
}
```

6. Performance Benefits

Zero-Cost Abstractions: Rust's iterators compile down to efficient loops with no runtime overhead.

Avoiding Temporary Allocations: Operations like map and filter do not create intermediate collections.

Example of Compiler Optimization

rust

Copy code

```rust
fn main() {
    let nums = vec![1, 2, 3, 4];
    let sum: i32 = nums.iter().map(|x| x * 2).sum();
    println!("{}", sum); // Outputs: 20
}
```

Conclusion

The Iterator trait, combined with functional composition, allows developers to write clean, efficient, and expressive Rust code. Its lazy evaluation ensures computations are performed only when necessary, and the wide range of iterator methods enables powerful data transformations. By mastering iterators and functional composition, Rust developers can leverage the language's full potential for modern, functional-style programming.

5.3 Using Algebraic Data Types: Enums and Structs

Algebraic data types (ADTs) are a foundational concept in many programming languages, especially functional ones. In Rust, enums and structs serve as the primary tools for building ADTs, enabling developers to model complex data structures in a clean, safe, and expressive way.

1. What Are Algebraic Data Types?

ADTs are types created by combining other types. There are two main kinds:

Product Types: Combine multiple fields (e.g., structs).
Sum Types: Represent one of several variants (e.g., enums).
Rust's enums and structs allow developers to implement these patterns effectively.

2. Structs: Product Types

A struct in Rust groups related fields together, creating a single composite data type.

Defining a Struct

rust

Copy code

```
struct Point {
    x: f64,
    y: f64,
}

fn main() {
    let point = Point { x: 3.0, y: 4.0 };
    println!("Point: ({}, {})", point.x, point.y);
}
```

Types of Structs

Named Field Structs: Standard structs with named fields.

Tuple Structs: Structs with unnamed fields.

rust

Copy code

```
struct Color(u8, u8, u8);
let red = Color(255, 0, 0);
println!("Red: ({}, {}, {})", red.0, red.1, red.2);
```

Unit-Like Structs: Structs with no fields, often used for markers or zero-sized types.

rust

Copy code

```
struct Marker;
```

3. Enums: Sum Types

Enums represent a type that can take one of several variants. Each variant may have associated data.

Defining an Enum

rust

Copy code

```
enum Shape {
    Circle { radius: f64 },
    Rectangle { width: f64, height: f64 },
}
```

```
fn area(shape: Shape) -> f64 {
    match shape {
        Shape::Circle { radius } => 3.14 * radius * radius,
        Shape::Rectangle { width, height } => width * height,
    }
}

fn main() {
    let circle = Shape::Circle { radius: 2.0 };
    let rect = Shape::Rectangle { width: 3.0, height: 4.0 };

    println!("Circle area: {}", area(circle)); // Outputs: 12.56
    println!("Rectangle area: {}", area(rect)); // Outputs: 12.0
}
```

Enums with Variants

Enums can be used to express concepts like options, results, or commands:

Option: Represents optional values (Some or None).
Result: Represents success (Ok) or failure (Err).

4. Pattern Matching with Enums and Structs

Rust's pattern matching makes working with enums and structs more powerful and expressive.

Example with Enums

```rust
Copy code
enum Message {
    Text(String),
    Quit,
}

fn handle_message(msg: Message) {
    match msg {
        Message::Text(content) => println!("Message: {}",
content),
        Message::Quit => println!("Goodbye!"),
    }
}
```

Example with Structs

```rust
Copy code
struct Point {
    x: i32,
    y: i32,
}

fn describe_point(point: Point) {
    match point {
        Point { x, y } if x == y => println!("Point is on the diagonal."),
        Point { x, y } => println!("Point: ({}, {})", x, y),
    }
}
```

5. Combining Structs and Enums

Often, enums and structs are used together to model complex data hierarchies.

Example

```rust
Copy code
struct User {
    id: u32,
    name: String,
}

enum Event {
    Login(User),
    Logout(User),
    Error(String),
}

fn log_event(event: Event) {
    match event {
        Event::Login(user) => println!("User logged in: {}",
user.name),
        Event::Logout(user) => println!("User logged out: {}",
user.name),
        Event::Error(msg) => println!("Error: {}", msg),
    }
}
```

6. Benefits of Algebraic Data Types in Rust

Type Safety: Prevent invalid states by design.

rust

Copy code

```
enum Direction {
    North,
    East,
    South,
    West,
}
```

Readability: Enums and structs make the intent of your code clear.

Expressiveness: Pattern matching enables concise handling of complex cases.

Memory Efficiency: Rust optimizes enum and struct representations for performance.

7. Real-World Use Cases

Enums: Represent state transitions, error handling, or finite states.

Structs: Model complex entities like database records or configuration options.

Example: Command-Line Parser

```rust
Copy code
enum Command {
    Add { item: String },
    Remove { id: u32 },
    List,
}

fn execute_command(cmd: Command) {
    match cmd {
        Command::Add { item } => println!("Adding: {}", item),
        Command::Remove { id } => println!("Removing ID: {}", id),
        Command::List => println!("Listing all items."),
    }
}
```

Conclusion

Enums and structs are integral to Rust's ability to express algebraic data types. Structs combine multiple pieces of related data, while enums represent one of many possible states or variants. Together, they allow developers to design clean, safe, and expressive programs that leverage Rust's powerful type system and pattern matching capabilities.

5.4 Pattern Matching for Functional Design

Pattern matching in Rust is a powerful feature that allows developers to deconstruct and analyze data structures in a concise and expressive way. Inspired by functional programming paradigms, pattern matching is a central tool for writing clear, robust, and idiomatic Rust code.

1. What is Pattern Matching?

Pattern matching involves checking a value against a pattern and executing code based on the match. Rust's match statement and destructuring capabilities make this process highly expressive.

Basic Syntax
rust
Copy code
```
fn main() {
    let num = 3;

    match num {
        1 => println!("One"),
        2 => println!("Two"),
        _ => println!("Something else"), // `_` acts as a catch-all
    }
}
```

2. Using match for Control Flow

The match keyword enables exhaustive matching, ensuring all possible cases are handled. This feature improves both correctness and readability.

Example: Matching Enum Variants

```rust
Copy code
enum Color {
    Red,
    Green,
    Blue,
}

fn print_color(color: Color) {
    match color {
        Color::Red => println!("Red"),
        Color::Green => println!("Green"),
        Color::Blue => println!("Blue"),
    }
```

}

Example: Catch-All Patterns

The _ pattern acts as a wildcard, matching any value not explicitly handled.

rust
Copy code
```rust
fn main() {
    let number = 42;

    match number {
        1 => println!("One"),
        2..=10 => println!("Between 2 and 10"),
        _ => println!("Something else"),
    }
}
```

3. Destructuring with Patterns

Pattern matching can deconstruct complex data types like tuples, structs, and enums, allowing direct access to their contents.

Matching Tuples

rust

Copy code

```rust
fn main() {
    let point = (3, 4);

    match point {
        (0, 0) => println!("Origin"),
        (x, 0) => println!("On the x-axis: {}", x),
        (0, y) => println!("On the y-axis: {}", y),
        (x, y) => println!("Point: ({}, {})", x, y),
    }
}
```

Destructuring Structs

rust

Copy code

```rust
struct Rectangle {
```

```rust
    width: u32,
    height: u32,
}

fn main() {
    let rect = Rectangle { width: 10, height: 20 };

    match rect {
        Rectangle { width, height } if width == height =>
println!("Square: {}", width),
        Rectangle { width, height } => println!("Rectangle:
{}x{}", width, height),
    }
}
```

Destructuring Enums

rust
Copy code
```rust
enum Shape {
    Circle { radius: f64 },
    Rectangle { width: f64, height: f64 },
}
```

```rust
fn describe_shape(shape: Shape) {
    match shape {
        Shape::Circle { radius } => println!("Circle with radius: {}", radius),
        Shape::Rectangle { width, height } => println!("Rectangle: {}x{}", width, height),
    }
}
```

4. Conditional Matching with Guards

Pattern guards allow additional conditions to be specified alongside patterns.

Example: Guards in match

rust
Copy code
```rust
fn main() {
    let num = 5;

    match num {
```

```rust
        x if x % 2 == 0 => println!("Even number: {}", x),
        _ => println!("Odd number"),
    }
}
```

5. if let and while let for Simplified Matching

For cases where only one pattern is relevant, if let and while let provide concise alternatives to match.

Using if let
rust
Copy code
```rust
fn main() {
    let opt = Some(42);

    if let Some(value) = opt {
        println!("Value: {}", value);
    } else {
        println!("No value");
    }
}
```

Using while let

rust

Copy code

```rust
fn main() {
    let mut stack = vec![1, 2, 3];

    while let Some(top) = stack.pop() {
        println!("Popped: {}", top);
    }
}
```

6. Combining Functional Design and Pattern Matching

Rust's pattern matching enables a functional programming style by facilitating transformations and decision-making directly within constructs like iterators and closures.

Example: Matching in Iterators

rust

Copy code

```rust
fn main() {
    let numbers = vec![Some(1), None, Some(2), Some(3)];

    let result: Vec<_> = numbers
        .into_iter()
        .filter_map(|x| match x {
            Some(val) if val > 1 => Some(val),
            _ => None,
        })
        .collect();

    println!("{:?}", result); // Outputs: [2, 3]
}
```

7. Exhaustiveness and Safety

Rust's compiler ensures that match expressions cover all possible cases. This exhaustiveness check helps avoid runtime errors and ensures correctness.

Example: Compiler Error for Missing Cases

rust

```
Copy code
enum Direction {
    North,
    East,
    South,
    West,
}

fn move_in_direction(dir: Direction) {
    match dir {
        Direction::North => println!("Moving North"),
        Direction::East => println!("Moving East"),
        // Missing South and West will cause a compile-time
error
    }
}
```

8. Advanced Techniques

Binding with @

The @ symbol allows matching and binding simultaneously.

rust
Copy code
```rust
fn main() {
    let num = Some(10);

    match num {
        Some(x @ 1..=10) => println!("Matched: {}", x),
        _ => println!("No match"),
    }
}
```

Nested Patterns

Complex data structures can be matched using nested patterns.

rust
Copy code
```rust
enum Tree {
    Leaf(i32),
    Node(Box<Tree>, Box<Tree>),
}
```

```rust
fn main() {
    let tree = Tree::Node(
        Box::new(Tree::Leaf(5)),
        Box::new(Tree::Leaf(10)),
    );

    match tree {
        Tree::Node(left, right) => {
            if let Tree::Leaf(val) = *left {
                println!("Left leaf: {}", val);
            }
            if let Tree::Leaf(val) = *right {
                println!("Right leaf: {}", val);
            }
        }
        _ => println!("Not a node"),
    }
}
```

Conclusion

Pattern matching is a core feature in Rust that supports a functional approach to program design. By enabling the decomposition of data structures, matching on complex cases, and ensuring exhaustive checks, it fosters safe, concise, and expressive code. Combined with other Rust features like iterators and closures, pattern matching provides a versatile toolset for writing elegant and maintainable programs.

Chapter 6.

Advanced Functional Patterns in Rust

Rust, while not a purely functional language, offers powerful features that support advanced functional programming patterns. These patterns allow developers to write concise, expressive, and maintainable code, especially for complex transformations, error handling, and asynchronous operations.

1. Composition with Closures and Combinators

Closures in Rust can be composed to create pipelines of operations. Using combinators like .map(), .filter(), and .fold() on iterators enables clean and functional data processing.

Example

rust

Copy code

```rust
let numbers = vec![1, 2, 3, 4];
let result: Vec<_> = numbers
    .into_iter()
    .filter(|x| x % 2 == 0)
    .map(|x| x * x)
    .collect();

println!("{:?}", result); // Outputs: [4, 16]
```

2. Monadic Patterns with Option and Result

Rust's Option and Result types embody monadic principles, enabling chaining of operations to handle optional values and errors without explicit branching.

Example: Chaining with Option

rust

Copy code

```rust
fn parse_number(input: &str) -> Option<i32> {
    input.parse().ok()
}


let result = parse_number("42")
    .and_then(|x| Some(x * 2));


println!("{:?}", result); // Outputs: Some(84)
```

Example: Error Propagation with Result
rust
Copy code
```rust
fn divide(a: i32, b: i32) -> Result<i32, &'static str> {
    if b == 0 {
        Err("Division by zero")
    } else {
        Ok(a / b)
    }
}


let result = divide(10, 2)
    .and_then(|x| divide(x, 0))
    .unwrap_or_else(|err| {
```

```rust
    println!("Error: {}", err);
    0
});
```

```rust
println!("{}", result); // Outputs: 0
```

3. Immutable State with Persistent Data Structures

Functional programming often emphasizes immutability. While Rust doesn't natively support persistent data structures, crates like im provide implementations for immutable collections.

Example

rust
Copy code
```rust
use im::Vector;

let vec = Vector::new();
let vec2 = vec.push_back(1);
println!("{:?}", vec); // Original vector remains unchanged
println!("{:?}", vec2); // Outputs: [1]
```

4. Pattern Matching and Algebraic Data Types

Using enums and pattern matching enables functional design patterns like sum types and exhaustive case handling.

Example

```rust
Copy code
enum Operation {
    Add(i32, i32),
    Multiply(i32, i32),
}

fn evaluate(op: Operation) -> i32 {
    match op {
        Operation::Add(a, b) => a + b,
        Operation::Multiply(a, b) => a * b,
    }
}
```

```rust
let result = evaluate(Operation::Add(3, 5));
println!("{}", result); // Outputs: 8
```

5. Lazy Evaluation with Iterators

Rust's iterators are lazy, enabling functional pipelines that don't compute values until needed, improving performance and efficiency.

Example
rust
Copy code
```rust
let numbers = 1..;
let result: Vec<_> = numbers
    .filter(|x| x % 2 == 0)
    .take(5)
    .collect();

println!("{:?}", result); // Outputs: [2, 4, 6, 8, 10]
```

6. Functional Error Handling with Combinators

Combinators like map_err and unwrap_or_else provide a functional way to handle errors.

Example

rust
Copy code

```
fn parse(input: &str) -> Result<i32, &'static str> {
    input.parse().map_err(|_| "Invalid number")
}

let result = parse("42")
    .map(|x| x * 2)
    .unwrap_or_else(|err| {
        println!("Error: {}", err);
        0
    });

println!("{}", result); // Outputs: 84
```

7. Concurrency with Functional Tools

Rust's asynchronous programming model can also adopt functional patterns, using combinators on futures.

Example

```rust
Copy code
use tokio::time::{sleep, Duration};

async fn fetch_data() -> Result<String, &'static str> {
    sleep(Duration::from_secs(1)).await;
    Ok("Data fetched".to_string())
}

#[tokio::main]
async fn main() {
    let result = fetch_data().await.unwrap_or_else(|err| {
        println!("Error: {}", err);
        "Default data".to_string()
    });

    println!("{}", result);
}
```

Conclusion

Advanced functional patterns in Rust, such as monadic error handling, lazy evaluation, and combinator-based composition, enable developers to write expressive and efficient code. By leveraging these patterns, Rust blends the strengths of functional programming with its system-level capabilities, empowering developers to build robust and maintainable applications.

6.1 Monad Patterns: Option and Result Revisited

In Rust, the Option and Result types are foundational tools for handling optional values and errors. They embody monadic principles, enabling the composition of operations in a clean, functional style while ensuring safety and eliminating common bugs like null pointer dereferences or unhandled exceptions.

1. What is a Monad?

A monad is an abstraction from functional programming that encapsulates a computation context, allowing operations to be chained while maintaining context safety. In Rust:

Option encapsulates an optional value (presence or absence).
Result encapsulates a value or an error (success or failure).

Monads support chaining using combinators like map and and_then, which transform or pass values while preserving the context.

2. The Option Monad

The Option type is defined as:

rust
Copy code

```rust
enum Option<T> {
    Some(T),
    None,
}
```

Key Methods and Patterns

map: Transforms the contained value.
and_then: Chains another computation that returns an Option.
unwrap_or: Provides a default value if None.

Example: Transforming and Chaining with Option
rust
Copy code

```rust
fn parse_number(input: &str) -> Option<i32> {
    input.parse().ok()
}
```

```rust
fn double_if_even(number: i32) -> Option<i32> {
    if number % 2 == 0 {
        Some(number * 2)
    } else {
```

```rust
        None
    }
}

fn main() {
    let result = parse_number("42")
        .and_then(double_if_even)
        .unwrap_or(0);

    println!("{}", result); // Outputs: 84
}
```

3. The Result Monad

The Result type is defined as:

rust
Copy code
```rust
enum Result<T, E> {
    Ok(T),
    Err(E),
}
```

Key Methods and Patterns

map: Transforms the success value (Ok).

map_err: Transforms the error value (Err).

and_then: Chains another computation returning a Result.

unwrap_or_else: Provides an error fallback.

Example: Error Propagation with Result

rust

Copy code

```rust
fn divide(a: i32, b: i32) -> Result<i32, &'static str> {
    if b == 0 {
        Err("Division by zero")
    } else {
        Ok(a / b)
    }
}


fn main() {
    let result = divide(10, 2)
        .and_then(|x| divide(x, 0))
        .unwrap_or_else(|err| {
```

```rust
        println!("Error: {}", err);
        0
    });

    println!("{}", result); // Outputs: 0
}
```

4. Combinators for Composition

Option Combinators

filter: Retains the value if it satisfies a predicate.
or_else: Provides an alternative computation for None.

Example: Filtering with Option
rust
Copy code
```rust
fn main() {
    let value = Some(42);

    let result = value
        .filter(|&x| x % 2 == 0)
        .unwrap_or(0);
```

```rust
    println!("{}", result); // Outputs: 42
}
```

Result Combinators

or_else: Provides an alternative computation for Err.

unwrap_or_else: Supplies a fallback computation for errors.

Example: Mapping Errors with Result

rust

Copy code

```rust
fn parse_number(input: &str) -> Result<i32, String> {
        input.parse().map_err(|_| "Failed to parse
number".to_string())
}

fn main() {
   let result = parse_number("abc")
     .map_err(|err| format!("Error: {}", err))
     .unwrap_or_else(|err| {
        println!("{}", err);
```

```
        0
    });
```

```
    println!("{}", result); // Outputs: Error: Failed to parse
number, 0
}
```

5. Chaining Computations

The and_then method is a cornerstone for chaining monadic computations, making workflows concise and expressive.

Example: Nested Computations

rust
Copy code
```rust
fn to_uppercase(input: Option<&str>) -> Option<String>
{
    input.map(|s| s.to_uppercase())
}
```

```rust
fn main() {
```

```
let result = Some("rust")
    .and_then(to_uppercase)
    .unwrap_or("default".to_string());

println!("{}", result); // Outputs: RUST
}
```

6. Monad Laws and Guarantees

While Rust doesn't enforce formal monad laws, Option and Result align closely with functional monadic principles:

Identity: Wrapping and unwrapping a value preserves the original.
Composition: Chaining functions produces the same result as applying them sequentially.

Example: Identity Law

rust
Copy code
```
let x = Some(42);
```

```
assert_eq!(x.and_then(Some), x); // Identity holds
```

7. Practical Benefits

Safety: Eliminates null and unhandled exceptions.
Expressiveness: Simplifies error handling and conditional logic.
Composable: Encourages chaining and declarative programming.

Conclusion

The Option and Result types exemplify monadic patterns in Rust, offering robust abstractions for handling optional values and errors. By leveraging combinators like map, and_then, and unwrap_or_else, developers can write safe, expressive, and composable code. These monadic patterns align well with Rust's goals of safety and reliability, making them indispensable tools for functional programming in the language.

6.2 Functors, Applicatives, and Composition in Rust

Rust's type system and functional programming features make it a great environment to explore abstractions like functors, applicatives, and composition. While Rust doesn't explicitly define these concepts, they are present in its combinators and functional constructs like Option, Result, and Iterator.

1. Functors in Rust

A functor is any type that can be mapped over. In Rust, functors are represented by types that implement methods like map, allowing you to apply a function to their contained values while preserving the structure.

Key Properties of Functors

Identity: Mapping the identity function over a functor should not change its value.

Composition: Mapping a composition of two functions is equivalent to mapping them one after the other.

Examples of Functors in Rust

Option

rust

Copy code

```rust
fn main() {
    let value = Some(42);
    let result = value.map(|x| x * 2);
    println!("{:?}", result); // Outputs: Some(84)
}
```

Result

rust

Copy code

```rust
fn main() {
    let value: Result<i32, &str> = Ok(42);
    let result = value.map(|x| x + 1);
```

```rust
    println!("{:?}", result); // Outputs: Ok(43)
}
```

Iterator

rust
Copy code
```rust
fn main() {
    let numbers = vec![1, 2, 3];
    let result: Vec<_> = numbers.iter().map(|x| x *
2).collect();
    println!("{:?}", result); // Outputs: [2, 4, 6]
}
```

2. Applicatives in Rust

An applicative extends a functor by allowing functions that themselves are wrapped in a context to be applied to values within another context. In Rust, this is commonly seen in methods like and_then (or flat_map for iterators).

Key Properties of Applicatives

Identity: Wrapping a value in a context and applying it is equivalent to the value itself.

Homomorphism: Applying a plain function within a context is the same as mapping that function directly.

Examples of Applicatives in Rust

Option

rust
Copy code

```rust
fn add(a: i32, b: i32) -> i32 {
    a + b
}

fn main() {
    let a = Some(2);
    let b = Some(3);
    let result = a.and_then(|x| b.map(|y| add(x, y)));
    println!("{:?}", result); // Outputs: Some(5)
}
```

Result

rust

Copy code

```rust
fn divide(a: i32, b: i32) -> Result<i32, &'static str> {
    if b == 0 {
        Err("Division by zero")
    } else {
        Ok(a / b)
    }
}

fn main() {
    let a = Ok(10);
    let b = Ok(2);
    let result = a.and_then(|x| b.map(|y| x / y));
    println!("{:?}", result); // Outputs: Ok(5)
}
```

3. Function Composition in Rust

Function composition combines multiple functions into a single function, enabling a more declarative style of programming. In Rust, closures and combinators facilitate this.

Composing Functions

rust

Copy code

```
fn double(x: i32) -> i32 {
    x * 2
}

fn add_one(x: i32) -> i32 {
    x + 1
}

fn main() {
    let compose = |x| add_one(double(x));
    println!("{}", compose(5)); // Outputs: 11
}
```

Composing with Iterators

rust

Copy code

```rust
fn main() {
    let numbers = vec![1, 2, 3];
    let result: Vec<_> = numbers
        .iter()
        .map(|x| x * 2)
        .filter(|x| x > 3)
        .collect();

    println!("{:?}", result); // Outputs: [4, 6]
}
```

4. Combining Functors, Applicatives, and Composition

Rust allows you to combine these concepts for more expressive and declarative code. Using Option and Result as examples, you can chain and compose computations safely.

Chaining Operations
rust
Copy code
```rust
fn double(x: i32) -> Option<i32> {
    Some(x * 2)
```

```rust
}

fn add_one(x: i32) -> Option<i32> {
    Some(x + 1)
}

fn main() {
    let result = Some(3).and_then(double).and_then(add_one);
    println!("{:?}", result); // Outputs: Some(7)
}
```

Error Handling with Composition

rust
Copy code
```rust
fn parse_number(input: &str) -> Result<i32, &'static str> {
    input.parse().map_err(|_| "Invalid number")
}

fn double(x: i32) -> Result<i32, &'static str> {
    Ok(x * 2)
}
```

```
fn main() {
    let result = parse_number("42").and_then(double);
    println!("{:?}", result); // Outputs: Ok(84)
}
```

5. Practical Benefits of These Abstractions in Rust

Expressiveness: Code becomes declarative and easier to reason about.

Safety: Contexts like Option and Result ensure correctness by preventing null values and unhandled errors.

Reusability: Functions and operations can be modular and composable.

Efficiency: Rust's zero-cost abstractions ensure these patterns don't incur runtime overhead.

Conclusion

By leveraging functors (map), applicatives (and_then), and composition, Rust developers can write expressive and maintainable code while benefiting from the language's strong safety guarantees. These abstractions, though rooted in functional programming, fit seamlessly into Rust's ecosystem, enabling powerful and concise workflows for handling data transformations, optional values, and error handling.

6.3 Creating Lazy Evaluations and Streams

Lazy evaluation is a programming paradigm where expressions are not immediately evaluated but deferred until their values are needed. This approach can improve performance by avoiding unnecessary computations and handling potentially infinite data structures. Rust, with its efficient iterator trait and combinators, naturally supports lazy evaluations and enables the creation of streams for processing data in a lazy, efficient manner.

1. What is Lazy Evaluation?

In lazy evaluation:

Expressions are computed only when their results are required.

It allows for the definition and manipulation of infinite sequences.

It avoids unnecessary calculations, saving computational resources.

Rust supports lazy evaluation primarily through iterators. Iterators in Rust do not compute results immediately; instead, they are evaluated when consumed.

2. Lazy Evaluation with Rust Iterators

Rust's Iterator trait is central to its lazy evaluation mechanism. Iterator methods like map, filter, and take are lazy—they describe what should happen but do not perform any computation until a terminal operation like collect or fold is called.

Example: Lazily Transforming Data
rust
Copy code

```rust
fn main() {
    let numbers = vec![1, 2, 3, 4, 5];

    // Lazily map and filter the iterator
    let lazy_result = numbers
        .iter()
        .map(|x| x * 2)    // Double each value
        .filter(|x| x > 5) // Keep only values greater than 5
        .take(2);          // Take the first two values

    // Materialize the result
    let result: Vec<_> = lazy_result.collect();
    println!("{:?}", result); // Outputs: [6, 8]
}
```

3. Streams and Infinite Sequences

Streams represent potentially infinite sequences of data. Using iterators, Rust can represent and work with such sequences efficiently.

Example: Generating Infinite Sequences
rust

```
fn main() {
    let infinite_numbers = (1..).map(|x| x * x); // Squares of
natural numbers

    // Lazily take the first 5 values
    let result: Vec<_> = infinite_numbers.take(5).collect();
    println!("{:?}", result); // Outputs: [1, 4, 9, 16, 25]
}
```

4. Key Lazy Evaluation Methods in Rust

map: Transforms each item lazily.

filter: Filters items based on a predicate lazily.

take: Limits the number of items lazily.

skip: Skips the first N items lazily.

chain: Combines two iterators lazily.

zip: Combines two iterators into pairs lazily.

Example: Combining Lazy Methods

rust

```rust
fn main() {
    let odds = (1..).filter(|x| x % 2 != 0); // Infinite odd numbers

    // Chain and process
    let result: Vec<_> = odds.take(5).map(|x| x * 3).collect();
    println!("{:?}", result); // Outputs: [3, 9, 15, 21, 27]
}
```

5. Performance Benefits of Lazy Evaluation

Reduced Memory Usage: Only the data currently needed is processed, avoiding large intermediate collections.
Improved Speed: Eliminates unnecessary calculations.
Infinite Structures: Allows working with data that cannot fit in memory (e.g., streams of real-time data).

Example: Avoiding Unnecessary Computation

rust
Copy code
```rust
fn main() {
    let result: Vec<_> = (1..)
```

```rust
    .filter(|x| x % 2 == 0) // Filter even numbers
    .take(3)         // Take only the first three
    .collect();      // Materialize the result

    println!("{:?}", result); // Outputs: [2, 4, 6]
}
```

6. Custom Lazy Iterators

You can implement custom lazy iterators by defining the Iterator trait.

Example: Creating a Lazy Fibonacci Sequence
rust
Copy code
```rust
struct Fibonacci {
    curr: u64,
    next: u64,
}

impl Iterator for Fibonacci {
    type Item = u64;
```

```rust
    fn next(&mut self) -> Option<Self::Item> {
        let new_next = self.curr + self.next;
        let current = self.curr;
        self.curr = self.next;
        self.next = new_next;

        Some(current)
    }
}

fn fibonacci() -> Fibonacci {
    Fibonacci { curr: 0, next: 1 }
}

fn main() {
    let fib = fibonacci();

    let result: Vec<_> = fib.take(10).collect();
    println!("{:?}", result); // Outputs: [0, 1, 1, 2, 3, 5, 8, 13, 21, 34]
}
```

7. Streams with Async Data

Lazy streams are essential in asynchronous programming, where data arrives over time. Rust's futures and tokio crates support async streams for processing asynchronous data sources.

Example: Using async-stream

```rust
Copy code
use async_stream::stream;
use tokio_stream::StreamExt;

#[tokio::main]
async fn main() {
    let stream = stream! {
        for i in 1..=5 {

tokio::time::sleep(tokio::time::Duration::from_secs(1)).await;
            yield i * i; // Lazily emit squared values
        }
    };
```

```
stream.for_each(|val| async move {
    println!("Received: {}", val);
}).await;
}
```

8. Practical Use Cases for Lazy Evaluation

Data Pipelines: Processing large datasets incrementally.
Infinite Streams: Generating values on demand.
Real-Time Data: Handling asynchronous data streams like user events or network responses.
Optimization: Avoiding unnecessary computations in performance-critical systems.

Conclusion

Lazy evaluation and streams in Rust offer powerful tools for managing data processing efficiently and declaratively. Using iterators, you can implement complex pipelines while maintaining performance and safety. For asynchronous or real-time systems, Rust's support for lazy streams ensures that developers can handle large or infinite datasets effectively. These features align well with Rust's goals of performance, safety, and expressiveness.

6.4 Functional Error Handling with Combinators

Error handling is an essential aspect of programming, and Rust provides a robust system for managing errors without exceptions. Using functional programming techniques, Rust leverages combinators to make error handling expressive, concise, and safe. These combinators operate on the Option and Result types, enabling functional-style error management through chaining and composition.

1. What Are Combinators?

Combinators are higher-order functions that operate on values wrapped in contexts like Option or Result. Instead of explicitly handling errors with conditionals (e.g., if/match), combinators allow developers to transform, propagate, or handle errors functionally.

2. Key Combinators for Error Handling

For Option
map

Transforms the value inside Some, leaving None unchanged.

rust
Copy code
```rust
fn main() {
    let value = Some(42);
    let result = value.map(|x| x * 2);
    println!("{:?}", result); // Outputs: Some(84)
}
```

and_then

Chains computations that might also return Option.

rust

Copy code

```rust
fn double_if_positive(x: i32) -> Option<i32> {
    if x > 0 { Some(x * 2) } else { None }
}

fn main() {
    let value = Some(3);
    let result = value.and_then(double_if_positive);
    println!("{:?}", result); // Outputs: Some(6)
}
```

unwrap_or

Provides a default value if the option is None.

rust

Copy code

```rust
fn main() {
    let value: Option<i32> = None;
    let result = value.unwrap_or(0);
    println!("{}", result); // Outputs: 0
}
```

For Result

map

Transforms the Ok value, leaving Err unchanged.

rust

Copy code

```rust
fn main() {
    let value: Result<i32, &str> = Ok(42);
    let result = value.map(|x| x * 2);
    println!("{:?}", result); // Outputs: Ok(84)
}
```

map_err

Transforms the Err value, leaving Ok unchanged.

rust

Copy code

```rust
fn main() {
    let value: Result<i32, &str> = Err("Error occurred");
    let result = value.map_err(|e| format!("Custom: {}", e));
```

```
    println!("{:?}", result); // Outputs: Err("Custom: Error
occurred")
}
```
and_then

Chains computations that might also return a Result.

rust
Copy code
```rust
fn double_if_positive(x: i32) -> Result<i32, &'static str> {
    if x > 0 { Ok(x * 2) } else { Err("Negative number") }
}

fn main() {
    let value: Result<i32, &str> = Ok(3);
    let result = value.and_then(double_if_positive);
    println!("{:?}", result); // Outputs: Ok(6)
}
```
unwrap_or_else

Provides a fallback value by calling a closure if the result
is Err.

rust

Copy code

```rust
fn main() {
    let value: Result<i32, &str> = Err("Error");
    let result = value.unwrap_or_else(|_| -1);
    println!("{}", result); // Outputs: -1
}
```

3. Combinator Chaining

Using combinators, multiple operations can be chained together in a functional pipeline, making the code more declarative.

Example: Chaining Result Combinators

rust

Copy code

```rust
fn parse_number(input: &str) -> Result<i32, &'static str> {
    input.parse().map_err(|_| "Invalid number")
}

fn double(x: i32) -> Result<i32, &'static str> {
```

```rust
    if x > 0 { Ok(x * 2) } else { Err("Negative number") }
}

fn main() {
    let result = parse_number("42")
        .and_then(double)
        .map(|x| x + 1);

    println!("{:?}", result); // Outputs: Ok(85)
}
```

4. Using ? for Concise Error Handling

Rust's ? operator simplifies propagating errors. It works like and_then, returning the error immediately if encountered.

Example: Simplified Error Propagation

rust
Copy code
```rust
fn process_number(input: &str) -> Result<i32, &'static str> {
```

```rust
    let number = input.parse::<i32>().map_err(|_| "Invalid
number")?;
    if number < 0 {
        Err("Negative number")
    } else {
        Ok(number * 2)
    }
}

fn main() {
    match process_number("42") {
        Ok(result) => println!("Result: {}", result),
        Err(e) => println!("Error: {}", e),
    }
}
```

5. Functional Error Recovery

Using combinators like unwrap_or, unwrap_or_else, and
or_else, you can provide fallback values or alternate
computations for error recovery.

Example: Recovering from Errors

rust

Copy code

```rust
fn main() {
    let result: Result<i32, &str> = Err("Parse error");

    // Recover with a default value
    let recovered = result.unwrap_or(0);
    println!("{}", recovered); // Outputs: 0

    // Recover with a fallback computation
    let recovered = result.unwrap_or_else(|_| -1);
    println!("{}", recovered); // Outputs: -1
}
```

6. Advantages of Using Combinators

Conciseness: Avoid verbose error-handling code.

Expressiveness: Clearly express intent without nested conditionals.

Safety: Prevent common pitfalls like unhandled None or Err.

Composability: Combine multiple transformations and error-handling steps.

7. Common Use Cases for Functional Error Handling

Input Validation: Parsing and validating user input.

File I/O: Reading files safely while handling errors.

Network Operations: Managing errors in HTTP requests or socket communication.

Data Pipelines: Chaining operations with potential failure points.

Conclusion

Functional error handling with combinators makes Rust code more readable, modular, and expressive. By leveraging combinators like map, and_then, and unwrap_or_else, developers can handle errors

declaratively and efficiently. Combined with the ?
operator, these tools ensure robust and idiomatic error
management, perfectly aligning with Rust's philosophy
of safety and performance.

Chapter 7.

Concurrency and Functional Programming in Rust

Rust provides robust support for concurrency with a focus on safety and performance, making it a powerful tool for building concurrent systems. By combining Rust's concurrency model with functional programming principles, developers can write expressive, safe, and efficient code for handling parallel tasks and asynchronous operations.

1. Rust's Concurrency Model

Rust's ownership system prevents common concurrency issues like data races by ensuring:

Safe Memory Access: No mutable references can coexist with other references.
Thread Safety: Types like Send and Sync enforce safe sharing and transfer of data between threads.

2. Functional Programming in Concurrency

Functional programming techniques, such as immutability, pure functions, and higher-order functions, align naturally with concurrent programming. Immutable data ensures that threads can safely share data without synchronization overhead.

Example: Using Immutability in Threads

```rust
Copy code
use std::thread;

fn main() {
    let numbers = vec![1, 2, 3, 4, 5];
    let handle = thread::spawn(move || {
        let sum: i32 = numbers.iter().sum();
        println!("Sum: {}", sum);
    });

    handle.join().unwrap();
```

}

3. Functional Concurrency with Iterators

Rust's iterators can be parallelized using libraries like Rayon, which extends functional methods (map, filter) to concurrent execution.

Example: Parallel Iterator with Rayon
rust
Copy code

```
use rayon::prelude::*;

fn main() {
    let numbers = vec![1, 2, 3, 4, 5];
    let squares: Vec<_> = numbers.par_iter().map(|x| x * x).collect();
    println!("{:?}", squares); // Outputs: [1, 4, 9, 16, 25]
}
```

4. Asynchronous Functional Programming

Rust's async ecosystem, powered by libraries like Tokio and async-std, integrates functional programming with asynchronous concurrency. Future combinators (map, and_then) allow composition of asynchronous tasks.

Example: Functional Async with Futures

rust
Copy code
```rust
use tokio::time::{sleep, Duration};

#[tokio::main]
async fn main() {
    let tasks = vec![1, 2, 3];
    let results: Vec<_> = tasks.into_iter()
        .map(|x| async move {
            sleep(Duration::from_secs(x)).await;
            x * x
        })
        .collect();

    for result in futures::future::join_all(results).await {
        println!("{}", result);
```

```
    }
}
```

5. Advantages of Functional Concurrency in Rust

Safety: Rust's ownership and type system ensure race-free concurrency.

Composability: Functional abstractions like iterators and combinators simplify concurrent task management.

Scalability: Libraries like Rayon and Tokio efficiently utilize system resources for parallel and async tasks.

Conclusion

Concurrency and functional programming complement each other in Rust, offering a powerful paradigm for building safe and high-performance systems. By leveraging immutable data, higher-order functions, and Rust's concurrency tools, developers can create robust solutions for complex, parallel, and asynchronous workflows.

7.1 Asynchronous Programming with Futures

Asynchronous programming in Rust enables efficient handling of I/O-bound or time-consuming tasks without blocking the main thread. Rust's Future trait forms the foundation of its async ecosystem, allowing developers to write non-blocking code while maintaining high performance and system resource efficiency.

1. What is a Future?

A Future in Rust represents a value that might not yet be available but will be resolved at some point in the future. Futures are lazy and do nothing until they are explicitly awaited or executed within a runtime.

Key Characteristics of Futures:

Non-blocking: Operations run concurrently, freeing the thread for other tasks.

Poll-based Execution: The Future trait defines a poll method, which the executor repeatedly calls to determine readiness.

2. Defining Asynchronous Functions

Rust uses the async keyword to define functions that return a Future. The await keyword pauses the execution of the function until the future resolves.

Example: Basic Async Function

rust
Copy code
```rust
async fn fetch_data() -> String {
    "Hello, async world!".to_string()
}

#[tokio::main]
async fn main() {
    let result = fetch_data().await;
```

```rust
    println!("{}", result);
}
```

3. Combining Futures

Futures can be composed and combined using combinators like map, and_then, and join_all, or directly with async blocks.

Example: Combining Futures with join!

```rust
rust
Copy code
use tokio::time::{sleep, Duration};

async fn task_one() {
    sleep(Duration::from_secs(2)).await;
    println!("Task one completed");
}

async fn task_two() {
    sleep(Duration::from_secs(1)).await;
    println!("Task two completed");
```

```
}

#[tokio::main]
async fn main() {
    tokio::join!(task_one(), task_two());
}
```

4. Using Async Runtimes

Rust requires an asynchronous runtime, such as Tokio or async-std, to execute futures. These runtimes manage task scheduling and provide utilities for async file I/O, networking, and more.

Example: Using Tokio Runtime

```
rust
Copy code
use tokio::time::{sleep, Duration};

#[tokio::main]
async fn main() {
    sleep(Duration::from_secs(1)).await;
```

```rust
    println!("Executed after 1 second");
}
```

5. Functional Programming with Futures

Futures integrate seamlessly with functional programming paradigms through combinators and closures.

Example: Transforming Futures with map

```rust
rust
Copy code
use tokio::time::{sleep, Duration};

async fn fetch_data() -> Result<i32, &'static str> {
    sleep(Duration::from_secs(1)).await;
    Ok(42)
}

#[tokio::main]
async fn main() {
    let result = fetch_data().await.map(|value| value * 2);
```

```
    println!("{:?}", result); // Outputs: Ok(84)
}
```

6. Common Patterns in Asynchronous Programming

Async Streams: Work with sequences of values produced asynchronously using the Stream trait.
Error Handling: Combine Result with futures for robust error propagation.
Concurrency: Use utilities like join!, spawn, or select! for running multiple futures concurrently.

7. Benefits of Asynchronous Programming in Rust

High Performance: Efficient use of system resources without blocking threads.
Predictable Execution: The poll-based model ensures fine-grained control over task scheduling.
Integration with Functional Techniques: Compose and transform asynchronous tasks using functional combinators.

8. Example: Building an Async Web Client

rust

Copy code

```rust
use reqwest::get;

#[tokio::main]
async fn main() -> Result<(), reqwest::Error> {
    let response = get("https://www.rust-lang.org").await?;
    let body = response.text().await?;
    println!("Response body: {}", body);
    Ok(())
}
```

Conclusion

Asynchronous programming with futures is a powerful paradigm in Rust, enabling developers to write efficient, non-blocking code for I/O-bound tasks. By leveraging the Future trait, async runtimes, and functional combinators, Rust provides a comprehensive toolkit for building scalable and responsive applications.

7.2 Functional Concurrency Patterns

Functional concurrency patterns in Rust leverage the principles of functional programming—immutability, higher-order functions, and composability—combined with Rust's robust concurrency model. These patterns allow developers to write expressive and safe concurrent code for high-performance applications while avoiding common pitfalls like data races and deadlocks.

1. Immutability and Data Sharing

Functional programming emphasizes immutability, which eliminates the need for synchronization when sharing data across threads. Rust enforces immutability by default, making it easier to use shared data safely in concurrent programs.

Example: Sharing Immutable Data

rust

Copy code

```rust
use std::thread;

fn main() {
    let numbers = vec![1, 2, 3, 4, 5];
    let handle = thread::spawn(move || {
        let sum: i32 = numbers.iter().sum();
        println!("Sum: {}", sum);
    });

    handle.join().unwrap();
}
```

2. Map-Reduce Pattern

This pattern breaks down computations into independent tasks (map) and combines their results (reduce). Rust's iterators and libraries like Rayon enable parallelized map-reduce operations.

Example: Parallel Map-Reduce with Rayon

rust

Copy code

```rust
use rayon::prelude::*;

fn main() {
    let numbers: Vec<i32> = (1..=100).collect();
    let sum_of_squares: i32 = numbers
        .par_iter()        // Parallel iterator
        .map(|&x| x * x)    // Map step
        .sum();            // Reduce step
    println!("Sum of squares: {}", sum_of_squares);
}
```

3. Task Composition

Functional concurrency encourages composing tasks with higher-order functions and combinators like join!, select!, or custom functional pipelines.

Example: Task Composition with tokio::join!

rust

Copy code

```rust
use tokio::time::{sleep, Duration};

async fn task_one() {
    sleep(Duration::from_secs(2)).await;
    println!("Task one completed");
}

async fn task_two() {
    sleep(Duration::from_secs(1)).await;
    println!("Task two completed");
}

#[tokio::main]
async fn main() {
    tokio::join!(task_one(), task_two());
}
```

4. Functional Streams for Concurrency

Streams are analogous to iterators but work with asynchronous data. Rust's Stream trait enables handling sequences of data produced asynchronously.

Example: Streaming with tokio-stream

```rust
Copy code
use tokio_stream::{self as stream, StreamExt};

#[tokio::main]
async fn main() {
    let items = stream::iter(1..=5);

    items
        .for_each(|x| async move {
            println!("Processing: {}", x);
        })
        .await;
}
```

5. Fork-Join Concurrency

The fork-join pattern divides work into smaller tasks (fork) that run in parallel and then aggregates the results (join). Rust's concurrency model supports this pattern efficiently with libraries like Rayon and async runtimes.

Example: Fork-Join with Multiple Threads

rust

Copy code

```rust
use std::thread;

fn main() {
    let handles: Vec<_> = (1..=4)
        .map(|x| thread::spawn(move || x * x))
        .collect();

    let results: Vec<_> = handles
        .into_iter()
        .map(|handle| handle.join().unwrap())
        .collect();

    println!("Results: {:?}", results);
}
```

6. Functional Futures

Futures in Rust can be combined and transformed using functional combinators like map and and_then. This approach makes concurrent code more declarative and composable.

Example: Transforming Futures
rust
Copy code
```
use tokio::time::{sleep, Duration};

async fn compute(x: i32) -> i32 {
    sleep(Duration::from_secs(1)).await;
    x * x
}

#[tokio::main]
async fn main() {
    let result = compute(4).await.map(|x| x + 1);
    println!("Result: {:?}", result); // Outputs: 17
}
```

7. Parallel Pipelines

Concurrent data pipelines process streams of data in parallel. Rust's channels and async runtimes provide tools to build these efficiently.

Example: Parallel Data Pipeline with Channels

rust

Copy code

```
use std::sync::mpsc;
use std::thread;

fn main() {
    let (tx, rx) = mpsc::channel();

    let producer = thread::spawn(move || {
        for i in 1..=5 {
            tx.send(i).unwrap();
        }
    });

    let consumer = thread::spawn(move || {
        for received in rx {
            println!("Received: {}", received);
```

```
    }
  });

  producer.join().unwrap();
  consumer.join().unwrap();
}
```

8. Concurrency with Functional Libraries

Libraries like Rayon (for parallel iterators) and Tokio (for async programming) simplify functional concurrency patterns in Rust.

Example: Using Tokio for Concurrent HTTP Requests

```rust
Copy code
use reqwest;
use tokio;

async fn fetch_url(url: &str) -> Result<String, reqwest::Error> {
  let response = reqwest::get(url).await?.text().await?;
```

```rust
    Ok(response)
}

#[tokio::main]
async fn main() {
        let urls = vec!["https://www.rust-lang.org",
"https://docs.rs"];
        let tasks: Vec<_> = urls.iter().map(|&url|
fetch_url(url)).collect();

    let results = futures::future::join_all(tasks).await;
    for result in results {
        match result {
            Ok(content) => println!("Content length: {}",
content.len()),
            Err(e) => println!("Error: {}", e),
        }
    }
}
```

Advantages of Functional Concurrency in Rust

Safety: Rust's ownership model ensures data races are impossible.

Composability: Functional abstractions make it easy to build modular concurrent code.

Performance: Efficient use of system resources through zero-cost abstractions and async runtimes.

Clarity: Declarative pipelines and combinators improve code readability.

Conclusion

Functional concurrency patterns in Rust empower developers to write expressive, safe, and high-performance concurrent applications. By leveraging tools like immutability, higher-order functions, and powerful libraries like Rayon and Tokio, Rust combines the best of functional and concurrent programming paradigms to handle complex workflows with ease.

7.3 Safe Parallelism in Rust

Parallelism involves dividing a task into smaller units that run simultaneously across multiple threads or cores. Rust offers robust tools for achieving parallelism safely, ensuring thread safety without sacrificing performance. By leveraging Rust's ownership model, data races and undefined behavior are eliminated, making it easier to write reliable and efficient parallel code.

1. Why Rust is Ideal for Safe Parallelism

Rust's ownership and type system enforce strict rules about data access:

Ownership and Borrowing: Ensures data is either mutable and exclusive or shared and immutable.

Thread Safety Traits: The Send and Sync traits ensure safe data sharing and transfer between threads.

Zero-Cost Abstractions: High-level parallelism APIs in Rust compile down to low-level, efficient code.

2. Parallelism vs. Concurrency

Concurrency involves managing multiple tasks that can execute out of order or in parallel.
Parallelism focuses on executing tasks simultaneously, usually to improve performance.

3. Tools for Parallelism in Rust

3.1 The Standard Library

Rust's standard library provides primitives for parallelism:

Threads: Create and manage threads using std::thread.
Channels: Facilitate communication between threads with std::sync::mpsc.
Mutex and RwLock: Ensure synchronized access to shared data.

3.2 Rayon

Rayon simplifies parallelism by extending iterators to run tasks in parallel with minimal effort.

3.3 Async Ecosystem

Although more suitable for concurrency, Rust's async runtimes (e.g., Tokio) can be used for parallel I/O-bound tasks.

4. Examples of Safe Parallelism

4.1 Using Threads

```rust
Copy code
use std::thread;

fn main() {
    let handle = thread::spawn(|| {
        for i in 1..10 {
            println!("Thread: {}", i);
```

```rust
    }
});

for i in 1..10 {
    println!("Main: {}", i);
}


    handle.join().unwrap(); // Wait for the thread to complete
}
```

4.2 Using Mutex for Shared State

rust
Copy code
```rust
use std::sync::{Arc, Mutex};
use std::thread;

fn main() {
    let counter = Arc::new(Mutex::new(0));
    let mut handles = vec![];

    for _ in 0..10 {
```

```rust
        let counter = Arc::clone(&counter);
        let handle = thread::spawn(move || {
            let mut num = counter.lock().unwrap();
            *num += 1;
        });
        handles.push(handle);
    }

    for handle in handles {
        handle.join().unwrap();
    }

    println!("Result: {}", *counter.lock().unwrap());
}
```

4.3 Parallel Iterators with Rayon

rust
Copy code
```rust
use rayon::prelude::*;

fn main() {
    let numbers: Vec<i32> = (1..=100).collect();
```

```
let sum_of_squares: i32 = numbers
    .par_iter()      // Parallel iterator
    .map(|&x| x * x)    // Map step
    .sum();          // Reduce step

println!("Sum of squares: {}", sum_of_squares);
}
```

5. Best Practices for Safe Parallelism

Prefer Immutability: Immutable data eliminates the risk of race conditions.

Use Safe Sharing Tools: Use Arc and synchronization primitives like Mutex and RwLock for shared state.

Leverage High-Level Libraries: Libraries like Rayon abstract complex parallelism while ensuring safety.

Avoid Deadlocks: Ensure locks are acquired in a consistent order and released promptly.

Test Thoroughly: Parallel code can have subtle bugs that are hard to reproduce; write tests that simulate various scenarios.

6. Advantages of Rust's Parallelism Model

Safety by Design: Data races are prevented at compile time.

High Performance: Zero-cost abstractions ensure minimal overhead.

Expressive APIs: High-level libraries like Rayon make parallelism easy and intuitive.

Flexibility: From low-level thread management to high-level parallel iterators, Rust offers solutions for various use cases.

7. Limitations and Challenges

Learning Curve: Understanding ownership, borrowing, and concurrency concepts can be challenging.

Complexity: Designing and debugging parallel algorithms require careful planning.

Conclusion

Rust's approach to safe parallelism combines performance and reliability, making it a standout choice for writing parallel applications. By leveraging tools like threads, synchronization primitives, and libraries like Rayon, developers can write scalable and efficient parallel programs while maintaining the safety guarantees Rust is known for.

7.4 Building Concurrent Functional Pipelines

Concurrent functional pipelines are a design pattern where data flows through a series of transformations, often processed in parallel. This approach combines the clarity and composability of functional programming with Rust's powerful concurrency model, enabling efficient and scalable data processing.

1. Key Principles of Functional Pipelines

Immutability: Data remains immutable, with each transformation producing a new value.
Composition: Functions are composed into a sequence, where the output of one is the input to the next.
Concurrency: Independent stages of the pipeline run concurrently, maximizing resource utilization.

2. Tools for Concurrent Pipelines in Rust

2.1 Iterators and Rayon

The Rayon library allows parallel processing of iterators, making it easy to build concurrent pipelines.

2.2 Channels for Data Flow

Rust's std::sync::mpsc channels enable communication between stages in the pipeline.

2.3 Async and Streams

The Stream trait and async runtimes like Tokio support asynchronous pipelines for handling I/O-bound tasks.

3. Implementing Functional Pipelines in Rust

3.1 Sequential Functional Pipeline

```rust
Copy code
fn main() {
    let data = vec![1, 2, 3, 4, 5];
    let result: Vec<_> = data
        .iter()
        .map(|x| x * x)   // Square each number
        .filter(|x| x % 2 == 0) // Filter even numbers
        .collect();
    println!("{:?}", result); // Outputs: [4, 16]
}
```

3.2 Parallel Functional Pipeline with Rayon

rust
Copy code
```rust
use rayon::prelude::*;

fn main() {
    let data = vec![1, 2, 3, 4, 5];
    let result: Vec<_> = data
        .par_iter()      // Parallel iterator
        .map(|x| x * x)   // Square each number
        .filter(|x| x % 2 == 0) // Filter even numbers
        .collect();
    println!("{:?}", result); // Outputs: [4, 16]
}
```

3.3 Concurrent Pipeline with Channels

rust
Copy code
```rust
use std::sync::mpsc;
use std::thread;
```

```rust
fn main() {
    let (tx, rx) = mpsc::channel();

    // Producer thread
    let producer = thread::spawn(move || {
        for i in 1..=5 {
            tx.send(i).unwrap();
        }
    });

    // Consumer thread
    let consumer = thread::spawn(move || {
        for received in rx {
            println!("Received: {}", received);
        }
    });

    producer.join().unwrap();
    consumer.join().unwrap();
}
```

4. Async Pipelines with Streams

4.1 Using Async Streams

rust

Copy code

```rust
use tokio_stream::{self as stream, StreamExt};

#[tokio::main]
async fn main() {
    let data = stream::iter(1..=5);

    data.for_each(|x| async move {
        println!("Processing: {}", x);
    })
    .await;
}
```

4.2 Combining Async Pipelines

rust

Copy code

```rust
use tokio::time::{sleep, Duration};
```

```rust
async fn stage_one(x: i32) -> i32 {
    sleep(Duration::from_secs(1)).await;
    x * x
}

async fn stage_two(x: i32) -> i32 {
    sleep(Duration::from_secs(1)).await;
    x + 10
}

#[tokio::main]
async fn main() {
    let result = stage_one(5).await;
    let result = stage_two(result).await;
    println!("Result: {}", result); // Outputs: 35
}
```

5. Error Handling in Pipelines

Use combinators like map, and_then, or filter_map to handle errors within pipelines gracefully.

Example: Handling Errors

rust

Copy code

```rust
fn main() {
    let data = vec![Ok(1), Err("error"), Ok(3)];
    let results: Vec<_> = data
        .into_iter()
        .filter_map(Result::ok) // Filter out errors
        .map(|x| x * x)
        .collect();
    println!("{:?}", results); // Outputs: [1, 9]
}
```

6. Best Practices for Building Pipelines

Use Parallel Iterators: Libraries like Rayon simplify concurrent processing.

Leverage Channels for Flexibility: Use channels to decouple pipeline stages.

Prefer Async Streams for I/O: For pipelines involving asynchronous tasks, Stream is a natural fit.

Minimize Shared State: Favor immutable data to avoid synchronization overhead.

Benchmark for Bottlenecks: Use tools like criterion to identify and optimize slow stages.

7. Advantages of Concurrent Functional Pipelines

Scalability: Easily process large datasets by utilizing multiple threads or cores.
Modularity: Each stage can be developed and tested independently.
Readability: Functional composition makes pipelines easier to understand and maintain.

8. Example: Complex Data Processing Pipeline

rust
Copy code
```rust
use rayon::prelude::*;

fn main() {
    let data: Vec<i32> = (1..=100).collect();

    let result: Vec<_> = data
        .par_iter()              // Parallel iterator
```

```
        .map(|&x| x * 2)          // Double the value
        .filter(|&x| x % 3 == 0)    // Keep multiples of 3
        .collect();

    println!("{:?}", result);
}
```

Conclusion

Building concurrent functional pipelines in Rust allows for elegant, safe, and high-performance data processing. By combining functional programming principles with Rust's concurrency tools—such as Rayon, channels, and async streams—developers can create scalable pipelines that effectively utilize system resources while maintaining readability and safety.

Chapter 8.
Real-World Functional Applications

Functional programming (FP) techniques in Rust are not just theoretical—they offer practical solutions to real-world challenges. By leveraging immutability, composition, and concurrency, Rust allows developers to build robust and efficient applications. Below are some examples of how functional programming principles are applied in real-world scenarios.

1. Data Processing Pipelines

Functional programming excels in transforming and analyzing large datasets. Rust's iterators and libraries like Rayon enable parallel and efficient data processing.

Use Case: Log Processing
Challenge: Process millions of log entries to extract meaningful insights.

Solution:

Use iterators to parse logs line by line.

Filter, map, and aggregate data using functional composition.

Leverage Rayon for parallel processing.

Example Code

rust
Copy code
```
use rayon::prelude::*;

fn main() {
    let logs = vec![
        "INFO: User logged in",
        "ERROR: Database connection failed",
        "INFO: User logged out",
    ];

    let error_logs: Vec<_> = logs
        .par_iter()
```

```
    .filter(|&log| log.contains("ERROR"))
    .collect();

  println!("Error logs: {:?}", error_logs);
}
```

2. Reactive Systems

Functional programming patterns are widely used in reactive systems where events are processed asynchronously. Rust's Stream trait and async runtimes like Tokio are ideal for building event-driven applications.

Use Case: Real-Time Chat Application

Challenge: Handle messages from multiple users concurrently.
Solution:
Use asynchronous streams for receiving and broadcasting messages.
Compose stream transformations to filter or enrich messages.

Example Code

rust

Copy code

```rust
use tokio_stream::{self as stream, StreamExt};

#[tokio::main]
async fn main() {
    let messages = stream::iter(vec!["Hello", "Hi", "Ping",
"Pong"]);

    messages
        .filter(|msg| async move { msg.starts_with('P') })
        .for_each(|msg| async move {
            println!("Processed message: {}", msg);
        })
        .await;
}
```

3. Web and API Development

Rust's functional programming features are ideal for web applications, offering composability, error handling, and scalability. Frameworks like Actix and Axum make heavy use of FP principles.

Use Case: RESTful API

Challenge: Build a scalable and maintainable API with clear error handling.
Solution:
Use combinators like map and and_then for processing requests.
Handle errors gracefully with Result and Option.

Example Code

```rust
Copy code
use axum::{handler::get, Router};
use std::net::SocketAddr;

#[tokio::main]
async fn main() {
    let app = Router::new().route("/", get(handler));
```

```
let addr = SocketAddr::from(([127, 0, 0, 1], 3000));
println!("Listening on {}", addr);

axum::Server::bind(&addr).serve(app.into_make_service())
.await.unwrap();
}

async fn handler() -> &'static str {
    "Hello, Functional World!"
}
```

4. Financial Modeling and Simulations

Financial applications often involve complex calculations, which benefit from the immutability and composability of FP. Rust ensures accuracy and performance in such scenarios.

Use Case: Portfolio Optimization

Challenge: Optimize asset allocation for maximum returns under constraints.

Solution:

Model portfolios as immutable data structures.

Use functional transformations for calculations.

5. Machine Learning and Data Science

Functional programming simplifies the implementation of mathematical operations and data transformations. Rust's performance makes it a great choice for machine learning pipelines.

Use Case: Feature Engineering

Challenge: Preprocess and clean large datasets efficiently.

Solution:

Use iterators and combinators to transform datasets.

Parallelize computations for faster processing.

6. Game Development

Functional programming is increasingly used in game development for managing state and creating reusable logic. Rust's safety guarantees ensure bug-free code.

Use Case: Game AI

Challenge: Implement decision-making logic for NPCs.
Solution:
Use pattern matching and algebraic data types to represent states.
Compose pure functions for decision-making.

7. Compiler Design and Parsing

Functional programming principles are a natural fit for building parsers and compilers, thanks to their emphasis on immutability and recursion.

Use Case: Custom Domain-Specific Language (DSL)
Challenge: Build a DSL for configuring a system.
Solution:
Represent grammar using algebraic data types.

Use recursive functions to parse and evaluate expressions.

Example Code

rust
Copy code
```rust
enum Expr {
    Number(i32),
    Add(Box<Expr>, Box<Expr>),
}

fn eval(expr: Expr) -> i32 {
    match expr {
        Expr::Number(n) => n,
        Expr::Add(lhs, rhs) => eval(*lhs) + eval(*rhs),
    }
}
```

Conclusion

Rust's combination of functional programming techniques and systems-level performance makes it ideal for a wide range of real-world applications. By leveraging Rust's expressive syntax, type system, and concurrency tools, developers can solve complex problems efficiently while ensuring reliability and maintainability.

8.1 Designing a Functional Web API with Rust

Building a web API in Rust is a great use case for functional programming techniques. Rust's safety guarantees, powerful type system, and support for asynchronous programming make it an excellent choice for creating scalable and maintainable APIs. By incorporating functional principles, you can design an API that is robust, composable, and easy to extend.

Key Concepts for a Functional Web API

Immutability: Ensure that API handlers do not mutate shared state, reducing bugs and race conditions.

Composition: Break down API logic into smaller, reusable, and composable functions.

Error Handling: Leverage Rust's Result and combinators to handle errors functionally.

Asynchronous Programming: Use async/await for handling I/O-bound operations like database queries and HTTP requests.

1. Choosing the Right Framework

Several Rust web frameworks support functional design principles:

Actix Web: High-performance framework with asynchronous support.

Axum: Modern framework emphasizing modularity and composability.

Warp: Lightweight framework with powerful routing based on functional patterns.

2. Example: Building a Functional API with Axum

Here's a step-by-step guide to building a simple API using functional programming concepts:

Setting Up the Project

Initialize a new Rust project:

bash
Copy code
```
cargo new functional_api
cd functional_api
```

Add dependencies to your Cargo.toml:

toml
Copy code
```
[dependencies]
axum = "0.6"
tokio = { version = "1.0", features = ["full"] }
serde = { version = "1.0", features = ["derive"] }
serde_json = "1.0"
```

Defining a Model

Create a simple data model for your API:

rust
Copy code
```rust
use serde::{Deserialize, Serialize};

#[derive(Serialize, Deserialize)]
struct User {
    id: u32,
    name: String,
    email: String,
}
```

Creating Handlers

Design API handlers as pure functions that take input, perform transformations, and return results:

rust
Copy code
```rust
use axum::{Json, extract::Path};
```

```rust
use std::collections::HashMap;
use tokio::sync::RwLock;

type Db = RwLock<HashMap<u32, User>>;

async fn create_user(
    Json(user): Json<User>,
    db: axum::extract::Extension<Db>,
) -> Json<User> {
    let mut db = db.write().await;
    db.insert(user.id, user.clone());
    Json(user)
}

async fn get_user(
    Path(user_id): Path<u32>,
    db: axum::extract::Extension<Db>,
) -> Option<Json<User>> {
    let db = db.read().await;
    db.get(&user_id).cloned().map(Json)
}
```

Composing Routes

Compose your routes using functional patterns for clarity and modularity:

rust
Copy code
```
use axum::{routing::get, Router};
use std::sync::Arc;
use tokio::sync::RwLock;
use std::collections::HashMap;

#[tokio::main]
async fn main() {
    let db: Db = Arc::new(RwLock::new(HashMap::new()));

    let app = Router::new()
        .route("/users", axum::routing::post(create_user))
        .route("/users/:id", get(get_user))
        .layer(axum::AddExtensionLayer::new(db));

    axum::Server::bind(&"0.0.0.0:3000".parse().unwrap())
        .serve(app.into_make_service())
        .await
```

```
    .unwrap();
}
```

3. Error Handling with Functional Combinators

Use combinators like map, and_then, and or_else to manage errors cleanly:

rust
Copy code
```
async fn get_user(
    Path(user_id): Path<u32>,
    db: axum::extract::Extension<Db>,
) -> Result<Json<User>, axum::http::StatusCode> {
    let db = db.read().await;
    db.get(&user_id)
        .cloned()
        .map(Json)
        .ok_or(axum::http::StatusCode::NOT_FOUND)
}
```

4. Adding Middleware

Middleware can be used to add functional behavior, like logging or authentication:

rust
Copy code

```
use axum::{middleware, http::Request, response::Response};

async fn log_middleware<B>(req: Request<B>, next: axum::middleware::Next<B>) -> Response {
    println!("Received request: {:?}", req.uri());
    next.run(req).await
}

fn setup_routes() -> Router {
    Router::new()
        .route("/users", axum::routing::post(create_user))
        .route("/users/:id", get(get_user))
        .layer(middleware::from_fn(log_middleware))
}
```

5. Testing the API

Functional programming encourages isolated, testable functions. Use unit tests for handlers:

rust
Copy code
```rust
#[tokio::test]
async fn test_create_user() {
    let db: Db = Arc::new(RwLock::new(HashMap::new()));
    let user = User {
        id: 1,
        name: "Alice".to_string(),
        email: "alice@example.com".to_string(),
    };

    let response = create_user(Json(user.clone()),
axum::extract::Extension(db.clone())).await;
    assert_eq!(response.0.name, "Alice");
}
```

6. Expanding the API

Using functional programming principles, you can:

Add middleware for caching or rate limiting.

Use streams for real-time updates.

Compose advanced error-handling strategies.

Conclusion

By embracing functional programming in Rust, you can build a web API that is modular, efficient, and maintainable. Frameworks like Axum and Warp align naturally with these principles, enabling developers to design expressive and scalable APIs. With Rust's focus on performance and safety, functional APIs are not only elegant but also robust and reliable for production use.

8.2 Data Processing with Functional Pipelines

Functional pipelines are a powerful programming paradigm for transforming and analyzing data. In Rust, functional pipelines are implemented using iterators, combinators, and traits, enabling developers to write clean, modular, and efficient code. Rust's zero-cost abstractions ensure that these pipelines are as performant as imperative loops, while its strong type system and error handling make them robust.

Core Concepts of Functional Pipelines

Composition: Break down complex transformations into smaller, reusable functions. Compose these functions into a pipeline for sequential execution.

Immutability: Operate on immutable data, avoiding shared state and side effects.

Laziness: Process data only when needed, reducing unnecessary computations.

Parallelism: Leverage Rust's tools like Rayon to process data in parallel for increased performance.

Building a Functional Data Processing Pipeline

Example: Processing a Dataset

Consider a dataset of numbers. You need to filter out even numbers, double the remaining numbers, and sum them up.

rust
Copy code

```
fn main() {
    let data = vec![1, 2, 3, 4, 5, 6, 7, 8, 9, 10];

    let result: i32 = data
        .into_iter()
        .filter(|&x| x % 2 != 0) // Keep odd numbers
        .map(|x| x * 2)      // Double each number
        .sum();              // Sum the results

    println!("The result is: {}", result); // Output: 50
}
```

Key Components of the Pipeline

filter: Filters elements based on a predicate.
map: Transforms each element using a function.
sum: Consumes the iterator and aggregates results.

Advanced Functional Pipelines

1. Chaining Multiple Transformations

Pipelines can handle complex transformations by chaining multiple steps.

Example: Processing Logs

rust
Copy code
```
fn main() {
    let logs = vec![
        "INFO: User logged in",
        "ERROR: Failed to connect to DB",
        "INFO: User logged out",
        "ERROR: Timeout occurred",
    ];

    let error_messages: Vec<_> = logs
        .into_iter()
```

```rust
    .filter(|log| log.starts_with("ERROR")) // Keep only error logs
    .map(|log| log.replace("ERROR: ", "")) // Remove the prefix
    .collect();                            // Collect results into a vector

    println!("{:?}", error_messages); // Output: ["Failed to connect to DB", "Timeout occurred"]
}
```

2. Laziness and Efficiency

Rust's iterators are lazy, meaning they process data only when the final result is needed. This avoids unnecessary computations and improves performance.

Example: Processing a Large Range Lazily

rust
Copy code
```rust
fn main() {
    let large_range = 1..1_000_000;
```

```rust
let result: u64 = large_range
    .filter(|&x| x % 7 == 0)  // Divisible by 7
    .map(|x| x * x)        // Square each number
    .take(5)               // Take the first 5 results
    .sum();                // Sum them up

    println!("The result is: {}", result);
}
```

3. Parallel Data Processing

Using the Rayon library, you can parallelize pipelines for faster execution on large datasets.

Example: Parallel Processing

rust
Copy code

```rust
use rayon::prelude::*;

fn main() {
    let data = (1..1_000_000).collect::<Vec<_>>();
```

```
let result: u64 = data
    .par_iter()          // Parallel iterator
    .filter(|&&x| x % 7 == 0)
    .map(|&x| x * x)
    .sum();

    println!("The sum of squares is: {}", result);
}
```

Real-World Applications

1. Data Analytics

Functional pipelines are ideal for aggregating and analyzing data:

Example: Calculate average sales from a dataset of transactions.

2. Text Processing

Transform and clean large volumes of text:

Example: Extract specific fields from CSV or JSON files using libraries like serde.

3. Machine Learning Pipelines

Prepare datasets by applying transformations and filtering:

Example: Normalize numerical features or encode categorical variables.

4. Log Analysis

Filter, aggregate, and analyze logs to detect patterns or anomalies:

Example: Extract error messages from server logs for monitoring.

Error Handling in Pipelines

Use combinators like and_then and unwrap_or to manage errors without breaking the pipeline.

Example: Handling Parsing Errors

rust
Copy code
```rust
fn main() {
    let data = vec!["42", "93", "invalid", "78"];

    let results: Vec<_> = data
        .into_iter()
        .filter_map(|x| x.parse::<i32>().ok()) // Ignore parse errors
        .collect();

    println!("{:?}", results); // Output: [42, 93, 78]
}
```

Conclusion

Functional pipelines in Rust enable expressive and efficient data processing. By chaining transformations, leveraging laziness, and using parallelism when needed, developers can handle large datasets with ease. Rust's type system ensures correctness, while its iterator-based model provides both clarity and performance, making it an excellent choice for modern data processing tasks.

8.3 Building a CLI Application Using Functional Techniques

Command-Line Interface (CLI) applications are a common use case for Rust due to its speed, safety, and robust tooling ecosystem. By incorporating functional programming techniques, CLI applications can be more modular, maintainable, and expressive. Rust's strong type system, pattern matching, and iterator-based functional constructs simplify complex workflows while ensuring runtime efficiency.

Why Functional Techniques for CLI Applications?

Composability: Break down functionality into smaller, reusable functions for better maintainability.

Immutability: Reduce bugs by working with immutable data structures.

Error Handling: Use Result and combinators for robust error management.

Data Transformation: Process and manipulate input/output data effectively using iterators and functional pipelines.

Steps to Build a Functional CLI Application

1. Setting Up the Project

Initialize a new Rust project:

bash
Copy code

```
cargo new functional_cli
cd functional_cli
```

Add dependencies for CLI argument parsing and utilities:

toml
Copy code
```
[dependencies]
clap = { version = "4.0", features = ["derive"] }
serde = { version = "1.0", features = ["derive"] }
serde_json = "1.0"
```

2. Define CLI Structure with Clap

Use clap to define the CLI's arguments and options.

rust
Copy code
```
use clap::Parser;

/// A simple CLI application to process data
#[derive(Parser)]
```

```
#[command(name = "functional-cli")]
#[command(about = "A CLI app built with functional
techniques", long_about = None)]
struct Cli {
    /// Input file
    #[arg(short, long)]
    input: String,

    /// Output file
    #[arg(short, long)]
    output: String,

    /// Filter condition
    #[arg(short, long)]
    filter: Option<String>,
}

fn main() {
    let cli = Cli::parse();

    println!("Input file: {}", cli.input);
    println!("Output file: {}", cli.output);
    if let Some(filter) = cli.filter {
```

```rust
        println!("Filter condition: {}", filter);
    }
}
```

3. Processing Input Data Functionally

Read and process the input file using functional pipelines:

```rust
rust
Copy code
use std::fs;
use std::io::{self, BufRead};

fn process_file(file_path: &str, filter: Option<&str>) ->
io::Result<Vec<String>> {
    let file = fs::File::open(file_path)?;
    let reader = io::BufReader::new(file);

    let lines: Vec<String> = reader
        .lines()
            .filter_map(Result::ok) // Ignore lines that can't be
read
```

```rust
        .filter(|line| {
            if let Some(filter) = filter {
                line.contains(filter) // Apply filter if specified
            } else {
                true // Keep all lines if no filter is provided
            }
        })
        .collect();

    Ok(lines)
}
```

4. Writing Output Functionally

Write processed data to an output file:

rust
Copy code
```rust
fn write_output(file_path: &str, data: &[String]) -> io::Result<()> {
    let content = data.join("\n");
    fs::write(file_path, content)
}
```

5. Combining Functionality

Integrate processing and writing into a single functional pipeline:

```rust
Copy code
fn main() -> io::Result<()> {
    let cli = Cli::parse();

    let processed_data = process_file(&cli.input,
cli.filter.as_deref())?;
    write_output(&cli.output, &processed_data)?;

    println!("Processed data written to {}", cli.output);
    Ok(())
}
```

Advanced Functional Features for CLI Applications

1. Parallel Data Processing

For large input files, use Rayon for parallel data processing.

rust
Copy code
```rust
use rayon::prelude::*;

fn process_file_parallel(file_path: &str, filter: Option<&str>) -> io::Result<Vec<String>> {
    let file = fs::File::open(file_path)?;
    let reader = io::BufReader::new(file);

    let lines: Vec<String> = reader
        .lines()
        .par_bridge() // Convert to parallel iterator
        .filter_map(Result::ok)
        .filter(|line| {
            if let Some(filter) = filter {
                line.contains(filter)
            } else {
                true
            }
        })
```

```
    .collect();

  Ok(lines)
}
```

2. Error Handling with Combinators

Use combinators like map, and_then, and or_else for error handling:

rust
Copy code
```
fn safe_parse(input: &str) -> Result<i32, String> {
  input
    .parse::<i32>()
    .map_err(|_| format!("Failed to parse '{}'", input))
}
```

3. Adding Unit Tests

Test individual functions for correctness and edge cases.

rust

```
Copy code
#[cfg(test)]
mod tests {
    use super::*;

    #[test]
    fn test_process_file() {
        let result = process_file("test_input.txt",
Some("filter")).unwrap();
        assert!(result.iter().all(|line| line.contains("filter")));
    }

    #[test]
    fn test_write_output() {
        let data = vec!["line1".to_string(), "line2".to_string()];
        write_output("test_output.txt", &data).unwrap();
        let output =
fs::read_to_string("test_output.txt").unwrap();
        assert_eq!(output, "line1\nline2");
    }
}
```

Conclusion

Building a CLI application with functional techniques in Rust enables clean, modular, and expressive code. Functional pipelines streamline data processing, while immutability and strong typing ensure robustness. By leveraging libraries like clap and integrating advanced features such as parallelism and combinators, you can create powerful CLI tools that are efficient, maintainable, and user-friendly.

8.4 Implementing Domain-Specific Languages (DSLs)

Command-Line Interface (CLI) applications are a common use case for Rust due to its speed, safety, and robust tooling ecosystem. By incorporating functional programming techniques, CLI applications can be more modular, maintainable, and expressive. Rust's strong type system, pattern matching, and iterator-based functional constructs simplify complex workflows while ensuring runtime efficiency.

Why Functional Techniques for CLI Applications?

Composability: Break down functionality into smaller, reusable functions for better maintainability.

Immutability: Reduce bugs by working with immutable data structures.

Error Handling: Use Result and combinators for robust error management.

Data Transformation: Process and manipulate input/output data effectively using iterators and functional pipelines.

Steps to Build a Functional CLI Application

1. Setting Up the Project

Initialize a new Rust project:

bash
Copy code

```
cargo new functional_cli
cd functional_cli
```

Add dependencies for CLI argument parsing and utilities:

toml
Copy code
```toml
[dependencies]
clap = { version = "4.0", features = ["derive"] }
serde = { version = "1.0", features = ["derive"] }
serde_json = "1.0"
```

2. Define CLI Structure with Clap

Use clap to define the CLI's arguments and options.

rust
Copy code
```rust
use clap::Parser;

/// A simple CLI application to process data
#[derive(Parser)]
```

```rust
#[command(name = "functional-cli")]
#[command(about = "A CLI app built with functional
techniques", long_about = None)]
struct Cli {
    /// Input file
    #[arg(short, long)]
    input: String,

    /// Output file
    #[arg(short, long)]
    output: String,

    /// Filter condition
    #[arg(short, long)]
    filter: Option<String>,
}

fn main() {
    let cli = Cli::parse();

    println!("Input file: {}", cli.input);
    println!("Output file: {}", cli.output);
    if let Some(filter) = cli.filter {
```

```rust
        println!("Filter condition: {}", filter);
    }
}
```

3. Processing Input Data Functionally

Read and process the input file using functional pipelines:

```rust
Copy code
use std::fs;
use std::io::{self, BufRead};

fn process_file(file_path: &str, filter: Option<&str>) ->
io::Result<Vec<String>> {
    let file = fs::File::open(file_path)?;
    let reader = io::BufReader::new(file);

    let lines: Vec<String> = reader
        .lines()
            .filter_map(Result::ok) // Ignore lines that can't be
read
```

```rust
    .filter(|line| {
        if let Some(filter) = filter {
            line.contains(filter) // Apply filter if specified
        } else {
            true // Keep all lines if no filter is provided
        }
    })
    .collect();

    Ok(lines)
}
```

4. Writing Output Functionally

Write processed data to an output file:

rust

Copy code

```rust
fn write_output(file_path: &str, data: &[String]) ->
io::Result<()> {
    let content = data.join("\n");
    fs::write(file_path, content)
}
```

5. Combining Functionality

Integrate processing and writing into a single functional pipeline:

```rust
Copy code
fn main() -> io::Result<()> {
    let cli = Cli::parse();

    let processed_data = process_file(&cli.input, cli.filter.as_deref())?;
    write_output(&cli.output, &processed_data)?;

    println!("Processed data written to {}", cli.output);
    Ok(())
}
```

Advanced Functional Features for CLI Applications

1. Parallel Data Processing

For large input files, use Rayon for parallel data processing.

rust
Copy code
```rust
use rayon::prelude::*;

fn process_file_parallel(file_path: &str, filter: Option<&str>) -> io::Result<Vec<String>> {
    let file = fs::File::open(file_path)?;
    let reader = io::BufReader::new(file);

    let lines: Vec<String> = reader
        .lines()
        .par_bridge() // Convert to parallel iterator
        .filter_map(Result::ok)
        .filter(|line| {
            if let Some(filter) = filter {
                line.contains(filter)
            } else {
                true
            }
        })
```

```
    .collect();

  Ok(lines)
}
```

2. Error Handling with Combinators

Use combinators like map, and_then, and or_else for error handling:

rust
Copy code
```rust
fn safe_parse(input: &str) -> Result<i32, String> {
    input
      .parse::<i32>()
      .map_err(|_| format!("Failed to parse '{}'", input))
}
```

3. Adding Unit Tests

Test individual functions for correctness and edge cases.

rust

```
Copy code
#[cfg(test)]
mod tests {
    use super::*;

    #[test]
    fn test_process_file() {
        let result = process_file("test_input.txt",
Some("filter")).unwrap();
        assert!(result.iter().all(|line| line.contains("filter")));
    }

    #[test]
    fn test_write_output() {
        let data = vec!["line1".to_string(), "line2".to_string()];
        write_output("test_output.txt", &data).unwrap();
        let output =
fs::read_to_string("test_output.txt").unwrap();
        assert_eq!(output, "line1\nline2");
    }
}
```

Conclusion

Building a CLI application with functional techniques in Rust enables clean, modular, and expressive code. Functional pipelines streamline data processing, while immutability and strong typing ensure robustness. By leveraging libraries like clap and integrating advanced features such as parallelism and combinators, you can create powerful CLI tools that are efficient, maintainable, and user-friendly.

Chapter 9.

Performance Optimization in Functional Rust

Functional programming in Rust provides a powerful approach to writing clean, expressive code. However, one of the primary concerns when adopting functional techniques is maintaining high performance. Rust's zero-cost abstractions, strict type system, and ownership model help ensure that functional patterns can be used without sacrificing performance. Here are several strategies to optimize performance in functional Rust:

1. Minimizing Allocations and Copying

Functional programming often involves immutable data and higher-order functions, which can lead to frequent allocations. To optimize performance, avoid unnecessary allocations:

Use & references instead of cloning or copying data when possible.

Leverage Cow (Clone on Write) for efficiently handling mutable and immutable data.

Avoid unnecessary Box or heap allocation by using stack-allocated types like arrays or slices.

Example:

```rust
Copy code
let data = vec![1, 2, 3];
let reference = &data; // Avoid unnecessary clone or allocation
```

2. Efficient Use of Iterators

Iterators in Rust are lazy, meaning computations are deferred until they are consumed. This allows you to chain operations without immediate computation, reducing overhead. However, careful attention should be given to:

Avoiding excessive intermediate collections: Use iterator methods like .map() and .filter() directly rather than collecting into temporary collections.

Using for loops for simple iteration to avoid unnecessary overhead from method chaining when not needed.
Minimizing boxing and cloning within iterator chains.
.Example:

rust
Copy code
```
let sum: i32 = (1..100).map(|x| x * x).filter(|&x| x % 2 == 0).sum();
```

3. Tail-Call Optimization (TCO)

Rust does not natively support tail-call optimization, which can be problematic for deep recursive functions. To mitigate stack overflow risks and improve performance:

Convert recursion to iteration using explicit loops when possible.

Use std::mem::replace or RefCell to manage state in a functional style without recursion.

Example (convert recursion to iteration):

rust
Copy code
```
fn factorial_iter(n: u64) -> u64 {
    (1..=n).fold(1, |acc, x| acc * x)
}
```

4. Parallelism and Concurrency

Rust's ownership system provides safety without needing a garbage collector, which is critical when optimizing for parallelism. You can safely use functional techniques in concurrent applications:

Parallel iterators with the rayon crate to parallelize operations without manual threading.
Concurrency with async/await for asynchronous tasks while maintaining a functional style.

Example:

rust

Copy code

```rust
use rayon::prelude::*;

let results: Vec<_> = (0..1000).par_iter().map(|x| x * x).collect();
```

5. Zero-Cost Abstractions

Rust emphasizes zero-cost abstractions, meaning that using higher-level abstractions, like iterators, closures, and pattern matching, won't incur performance penalties compared to lower-level operations. Always prefer idiomatic Rust, as it is designed to be as efficient as possible while maintaining safety and expressiveness.

Use Rust's built-in types like Option and Result to represent computations with minimal overhead.
Profile code using tools like cargo bench to identify bottlenecks before optimizing.

6. Efficient Memory Management

Functional code in Rust can sometimes lead to excessive memory usage due to immutability and complex data structures. To optimize memory usage:

Avoid unnecessary cloning by using references and smart pointers like Rc or Arc when ownership needs to be shared.
Use Vec over LinkedList for better cache locality and performance in most cases.
Avoid excessive indirection with Box or Rc when not required.

7. Inlining Functions

Inlining small functions can help reduce function call overhead. Rust does this automatically for simple functions, but using the #[inline(always)] attribute can further encourage the compiler to inline functions where appropriate.

Example:

rust

Copy code

```rust
#[inline(always)]
fn add(a: i32, b: i32) -> i32 {
    a + b
}
```

Conclusion

While functional programming techniques in Rust can sometimes introduce overhead due to immutability and recursion, they can be highly efficient when applied thoughtfully. By leveraging Rust's powerful performance features like zero-cost abstractions, parallelism, and efficient memory management, you can write functional code that is both expressive and performant.

9.1 Zero-Cost Abstractions in Functional Design

In Rust, zero-cost abstractions refer to the concept where high-level abstractions, such as functional programming patterns, do not incur a runtime performance penalty. This is one of the core design philosophies of the language, aiming to provide expressive and safe code without compromising performance. Rust achieves this through its powerful type system, ownership model, and advanced compiler optimizations.

In functional design, abstractions like higher-order functions, iterators, closures, and pattern matching are commonly used. The challenge is to maintain the efficiency of these abstractions without incurring unnecessary overhead. Here's how zero-cost abstractions apply to functional design in Rust:

1. High-Level Abstractions Without Runtime Cost

Rust allows the use of complex, high-level abstractions without adding performance overhead, as long as the abstractions are designed to be "zero-cost." This means that at runtime, the Rust compiler ensures that these abstractions are as efficient as their low-level counterparts.

Iterators: Rust's iterators are a prime example of zero-cost abstractions. You can chain multiple operations like map, filter, and fold without creating intermediate collections, and the Rust compiler will optimize the entire chain into a single, efficient loop.

Example:

rust
Copy code
```
let sum: i32 = (1..1000).map(|x| x * 2).filter(|&x| x % 3 == 0).sum();
```

This iterator chain is compiled into a single loop that performs the transformation and filtering on-the-fly without creating temporary collections.

2. Immutability and Borrowing with Zero Cost

Functional programming encourages immutability, which can introduce performance concerns, especially with frequent data copying. However, Rust's ownership system and borrowing model allow immutability with minimal runtime cost.

References and Borrowing: By borrowing data instead of copying it, Rust enables efficient memory usage. The & (immutable borrow) and &mut (mutable borrow) references allow you to pass data around without duplicating it, reducing the overhead usually associated with immutability in other languages.

Example:

rust
Copy code
```
fn print_length(s: &str) {
    println!("Length: {}", s.len());
}
```

Here, print_length borrows the string reference without copying or cloning the string, preserving both performance and safety.

3. Pattern Matching and Enum Handling

Pattern matching in Rust, especially with enums, is another area where zero-cost abstractions shine. The Rust compiler can optimize match arms and perform efficient branching, often turning what would be a series of costly runtime checks in other languages into direct jump instructions.

Enums and Matching: Using enums in functional design allows you to express complex data structures without paying a performance penalty. The Rust compiler can turn match expressions into highly efficient machine code. This is especially true for small enums or enums with just a few variants.

Example:

rust

```
Copy code
enum Result<T, E> {
    Ok(T),
    Err(E),
}

fn process_result(result: Result<i32, String>) {
    match result {
        Result::Ok(value) => println!("Success: {}", value),
        Result::Err(err) => println!("Error: {}", err),
    }
}
```

Rust can optimize the match expression above, removing any unnecessary runtime overhead when evaluating the enum variants.

4. Higher-Order Functions Without Performance Loss

Higher-order functions (HOFs) are fundamental to functional programming. In Rust, functions like map, filter, and fold are implemented as iterator adapters that leverage closures. Despite their high-level nature, these functions don't introduce performance overhead. Rust's ownership system and optimizations like monomorphization ensure that closures are compiled in a way that eliminates extra costs.

Monomorphization: When generic functions and closures are used, Rust's compiler generates specialized versions of these functions at compile time, avoiding the runtime overhead of dynamic dispatch.

Example:

rust
Copy code
```
let numbers = vec![1, 2, 3, 4, 5];
let doubled: Vec<i32> = numbers.iter().map(|&x| x * 2).collect();
```

The map and collect methods here are optimized by the compiler, and no dynamic allocations or runtime overhead are introduced.

5. Using Macros for Abstraction

Rust's macro system is a key component for implementing zero-cost abstractions. Macros allow you to define high-level abstractions in the form of reusable code patterns, which are expanded at compile time, leaving no runtime overhead.

Declarative Macros: Macros like println! and vec! create code that, when expanded, has no extra performance costs. This makes it possible to create abstractions like custom data structures or functional operations without slowing down execution.

Example:

```rust
Copy code
macro_rules! sum {
    ($($x:expr),*) => {
        {
            let mut total = 0;
            $(
                total += $x;
```

```
    )*
    total
  }
};
}
```

```
let result = sum!(1, 2, 3, 4);
println!("Sum: {}", result);
```

The macro expands into a normal for loop, and the resulting code is efficient with no runtime cost.

6. Zero-Cost Abstractions in Concurrency

Rust's concurrency model is another example of zero-cost abstraction. The ownership and borrowing rules allow for safe parallelism and concurrency without requiring a garbage collector or locking mechanisms that would typically introduce performance overhead.

Concurrency and Parallelism: Rust's approach to data ownership ensures that threads or tasks do not encounter race conditions or memory safety issues without the need for runtime checks.

Example using the rayon crate:

```rust
Copy code
use rayon::prelude::*;

let numbers: Vec<i32> = (1..1_000_000).collect();
let sum: i32 = numbers.par_iter().map(|&x| x * 2).sum();
```

Rust ensures that the parallel iteration doesn't add overhead beyond the necessary logic for parallel execution.

Conclusion

Zero-cost abstractions in Rust enable developers to build high-level, expressive, and safe functional code without sacrificing performance. Rust's combination of strict type safety, ownership system, compiler optimizations, and powerful abstractions like iterators, closures, and enums ensures that functional techniques can be applied without negatively impacting execution speed. By adhering to the zero-cost principle, Rust allows for the creation of efficient, high-performance functional code that remains easy to understand and maintain.

9.2 Profiling and Benchmarking Functional Code

In any programming paradigm, understanding the performance of your code is crucial to optimizing it effectively. This is especially true when adopting functional programming techniques, which often involve abstractions like iterators, higher-order functions, and immutability. While these abstractions help write expressive and concise code, they can sometimes introduce overhead. Profiling and benchmarking are essential tools for identifying performance bottlenecks and ensuring that functional code in Rust maintains the high-performance standards that the language is known for.

This section will explore how to profile and benchmark functional code in Rust, covering tools, techniques, and best practices.

1. Benchmarking in Rust

Benchmarking allows you to measure the execution time of specific pieces of code. In Rust, the primary tool for benchmarking is the Criterion crate, which provides high-precision benchmarking capabilities.

Setting Up Benchmarking with Criterion

To benchmark functional code, you first need to include the criterion crate in your Cargo.toml file:

toml
Copy code
[dev-dependencies]

criterion = "0.3"

Then, create a benches directory in your project root and add a benchmarking file (e.g., benches/my_benchmark.rs).

Example Benchmark

Here's an example of how to benchmark the performance of a functional approach like using iterators in Rust:

```rust
Copy code
use criterion::{black_box, Criterion};

fn sum_of_squares(nums: Vec<i32>) -> i32 {
    nums.iter().map(|&x| x * x).sum()
}

fn benchmark_sum_of_squares(c: &mut Criterion) {
    let nums: Vec<i32> = (1..1000).collect();
    c.bench_function("sum_of_squares", |b| {
```

```
        b.iter(|| sum_of_squares(black_box(nums.clone())))
    });
}
```

```
criterion_group!(benches, benchmark_sum_of_squares);
criterion_main!(benches);
```

In this example:

black_box is used to prevent the compiler from optimizing away the code you are benchmarking.
c.bench_function benchmarks the sum_of_squares function over several iterations.
black_box(nums.clone()) ensures that the input data is not optimized out during benchmarking.

Running the Benchmark

To run the benchmark, use the following command:

bash
Copy code
cargo bench

This will execute the benchmarks and provide detailed statistics, such as the average time per iteration and the variability in execution time.

2. Profiling Rust Code

Profiling goes a step beyond benchmarking by providing insight into where the program spends most of its execution time. It helps identify bottlenecks in your code, which is essential for optimizing performance, especially in functional designs.

Using perf for Profiling

perf is a powerful Linux tool for profiling and analyzing performance. To use perf in Rust, you first need to compile your Rust code with debug symbols and optimizations disabled to gather detailed performance data:

bash
Copy code
cargo build --release

After compiling the code, you can run perf on your application:

```bash
Copy code
perf record ./target/release/your_program
```

This command records performance data, which you can then analyze:

```bash
Copy code
perf report
```

This report will give you information on where your application spends time, such as CPU cycles used in specific functions or methods. It helps highlight inefficient areas in your functional code that could be optimized.

Using cargo-flamegraph for Flame Graphs

Another useful tool is cargo-flamegraph, which integrates with perf and produces flame graphs. Flame graphs visualize the stack trace, making it easier to identify performance bottlenecks in your code.

To install cargo-flamegraph, run:

bash
Copy code
cargo install flamegraph

Then, to generate a flame graph, use the following command:

bash
Copy code
cargo flamegraph

This will generate an interactive flame graph that shows the functions where your program spends the most time. It can help identify inefficiencies in functional abstractions like iterators, closures, or recursion.

3. Profiling Functional Constructs

When profiling and benchmarking functional code, it's important to understand how certain functional constructs can impact performance. Here are some common areas where functional programming patterns may need closer inspection:

Iterators and Lazy Evaluation

While iterators in Rust are generally very efficient, sometimes certain iterator chains can introduce performance penalties, particularly if you're unnecessarily creating intermediate collections or performing complex transformations.

Chaining Iterators: Each call to methods like .map(), .filter(), and .fold() creates an iterator that lazily applies the transformations. However, too many chained transformations can reduce efficiency. Profiling helps identify the most costly iterator steps.

Higher-Order Functions and Closures

Using closures and higher-order functions in Rust can result in efficient code, but they sometimes lead to additional allocations or dynamic dispatch if not properly optimized.

Closure Capture: Closures that capture variables by value (e.g., move closures) can lead to additional heap allocations. Profiling can highlight closures that introduce such overhead.

Inlining: If a closure is small and called frequently, it might be more efficient to inline it directly instead of passing it as a function pointer.

Recursion and Stack Usage

Recursion is a common functional pattern but can be inefficient in Rust due to the lack of tail call optimization. Profiling recursive functions can reveal performance bottlenecks related to deep recursion and stack usage.

Tail-Call Recursion: Rust does not support tail-call optimization by default, so deep recursion might lead to stack overflows. Profiling deep recursive calls can help identify potential stack issues.

Memory Allocation and Immutability

Functional programming in Rust often emphasizes immutability, which can result in more frequent allocations if not managed carefully. Profiling can help determine whether unnecessary memory allocations or copies are occurring in your functional code.

4. Best Practices for Profiling and Benchmarking Functional Code

Measure Before Optimizing: Always benchmark and profile first to ensure you are optimizing the right parts of your code. Premature optimization can lead to unnecessary complexity.

Isolate Hot Paths: Focus your benchmarking efforts on the "hot paths" of your program—the areas where performance improvements will have the most impact.

Use Practical Data Sets: Ensure you benchmark using realistic input sizes. For example, avoid testing performance with tiny arrays or single data points when you expect your program to handle much larger datasets in production.

Optimize Based on Findings: Use the insights from profiling to refine your functional code. This may involve simplifying complex iterator chains, avoiding unnecessary cloning, or optimizing recursive functions.

Conclusion

Profiling and benchmarking are critical steps when writing functional code in Rust. Even though functional abstractions like iterators, closures, and immutability are typically efficient, profiling allows you to identify performance issues and make data-driven optimizations. By using tools like Criterion, perf, and cargo-flamegraph, you can gain a deep understanding of where your functional Rust code spends time and improve its efficiency without sacrificing readability or safety.

9.3 Reducing Runtime Overheads in Rust Programs

Rust is a systems programming language designed to offer high performance, safety, and concurrency, all without sacrificing control over low-level details like memory management. However, even in a language like Rust, there can be runtime overheads if programs are not written efficiently. Understanding and reducing these overheads is critical to maintaining the high performance that Rust promises. This section explores strategies to reduce runtime overheads in Rust programs, focusing on key areas like memory allocation, abstraction, control flow, and concurrency.

1. Minimize Heap Allocations

Heap allocations are typically slower than stack allocations due to the additional cost of managing memory at runtime. To reduce heap allocations in Rust, consider the following strategies:

Prefer Stack Allocation: Rust's ownership and borrowing system encourage stack allocation for smaller, short-lived data. Whenever possible, use types like i32, f32, or bool directly instead of wrapping them in heap-allocated types like Box<i32>. For small or temporary data, stack allocation is much faster.

Example:

rust
Copy code
```
fn calculate() -> i32 {
    let x = 5; // Stack-allocated
```

```
    let y = 10; // Stack-allocated
    x + y
}
```

Use Copy Types: Rust's Copy types, such as integers and simple structs, don't require heap allocations when passed by value. These types are implicitly copied, which can avoid costly allocations.

Avoid Unnecessary Cloning: The clone() method performs heap allocation, which can add unnecessary overhead. Instead, prefer borrowing data with references (&) and avoid cloning when it's not required.

Example:

```rust
Copy code
let s = String::from("Hello");
let reference = &s; // Borrow instead of cloning
```

Use Vec and Array Efficiently: In cases where you need dynamically sized collections, prefer using Vec<T>.

However, if the size of the collection is known ahead of time, use Vec::with_capacity to preallocate memory and avoid repeated reallocations.

Example:

```rust
Copy code
let mut vec = Vec::with_capacity(100);
for i in 0..100 {
    vec.push(i);
}
```

2. Efficient Abstractions

Rust encourages high-level abstractions like iterators, closures, and traits. While these abstractions help write expressive, maintainable code, they can sometimes introduce overhead. It's crucial to ensure that abstractions are efficient.

Iterators and Lazy Evaluation: Rust's iterators use lazy evaluation, meaning that computations are deferred until absolutely necessary. However, chaining too many iterator methods can sometimes introduce performance overhead due to the creation of intermediate iterators.

Minimize Iterator Chains: While Rust's iterators are designed to be efficient, complex chains of map(), filter(), and fold() can result in overhead due to multiple iterator objects being created. Profile your code and simplify iterator chains where possible.

Example:

rust
Copy code
```
let sum: i32 = (1..100).map(|x| x * 2).filter(|&x| x % 3 == 0).sum();
```

In this example, the multiple chained iterator methods are generally efficient, but for large datasets, you could simplify the logic into a more direct loop to avoid additional allocations.

Avoid Dynamic Dispatch: Rust's trait system allows for both static and dynamic dispatch. While dynamic dispatch (via trait objects) offers flexibility, it comes with a runtime cost due to vtable lookups. When performance is critical, use static dispatch by specifying the concrete type instead of using a trait object (dyn Trait).

Example of Dynamic Dispatch:

rust
Copy code
```rust
fn print_value(val: &dyn Display) {
    println!("{}", val);
}
```

Instead, prefer using generic functions to avoid dynamic dispatch:

rust
Copy code
```rust
fn print_value<T: Display>(val: T) {
    println!("{}", val);
```

```
}
```

3. Reducing Recursion Overhead

Recursion is a common functional programming technique, but in Rust, deep recursion can lead to stack overflow issues, especially when the compiler cannot optimize the recursion into a loop (i.e., tail-call optimization is not supported by default).

Convert Recursion to Iteration: In cases of deep recursion, try to convert recursive functions to iterative ones to avoid stack overflow and reduce overhead.

Example:

rust
Copy code
```rust
// Recursive version
fn factorial(n: u64) -> u64 {
    if n == 0 { 1 } else { n * factorial(n - 1) }
}
```

```
// Iterative version
fn factorial(n: u64) -> u64 {
    let mut result = 1;
    for i in 1..=n {
        result *= i;
    }
    result
}
```

Tail Recursion with std::mem::replace: Although Rust does not support automatic tail-call optimization, you can manually optimize tail-recursive functions by using an accumulator to hold intermediate results and avoiding stack growth.

4. Minimize Use of Box and Rc for Heap Allocation

Rust allows heap allocation through types like Box<T>, Rc<T>, and Arc<T>, which are useful in some scenarios, but they can introduce runtime overhead due to memory management (heap allocation and reference counting).

Prefer Stack Allocation: When possible, try to use stack-allocated types like Vec<T> or arrays instead of Box<T>. Only use heap allocation when absolutely necessary for your data structures.

Avoid Unnecessary Reference Counting: Rc<T> and Arc<T> are reference-counted smart pointers, which can introduce performance overhead because of atomic operations (for Arc) or non-atomic counting (for Rc). Use them when shared ownership is required but be mindful of the cost.

5. Concurrency and Parallelism Optimizations

Rust provides powerful concurrency primitives, but using them inefficiently can introduce significant runtime overhead. To minimize these overheads:

Avoid Excessive Thread Creation: While Rust makes it easy to spawn threads, creating too many threads can introduce overhead due to context switching. Use async/await or thread pools (e.g., rayon) to efficiently handle parallelism without the cost of creating excessive threads.

Leverage Work Stealing: For fine-grained parallelism, consider using Rust's parallel iterator library, such as rayon, which uses work-stealing algorithms to ensure threads aren't idly waiting for tasks.

Example:

```rust
Copy code
use rayon::prelude::*;

let sum: i32 = (1..1000).into_par_iter().map(|x| x * 2).sum();
```

Minimize Locking and Mutexes: Rust's ownership model prevents many common concurrency issues, but if you need shared access to mutable data, use locking mechanisms like Mutex or RwLock. However, excessive locking can introduce contention and slow down your program. Minimize lock contention by reducing the number of locks or using more fine-grained locks when appropriate.

6. Profile and Optimize Hot Paths

Profiling is key to understanding where runtime overheads occur in your Rust program. Use tools like perf, cargo-flamegraph, or Criterion to identify performance bottlenecks in critical sections of your code. After profiling, focus optimization efforts on the "hot paths"—the parts of the program that consume the most time.

7. Enable Compiler Optimizations

Rust's compiler provides optimizations that help reduce runtime overhead. To take full advantage of these optimizations, ensure you compile your code in release mode using:

bash
Copy code
cargo build --release

This will enable optimizations like inlining, loop unrolling, and dead code elimination that help make the code run faster.

Conclusion

Reducing runtime overheads in Rust programs is an essential part of writing high-performance code. By minimizing heap allocations, avoiding unnecessary abstractions, optimizing recursion, and leveraging efficient concurrency patterns, you can write programs that are both fast and maintainable. Profiling your code with tools like perf, cargo-flamegraph, and Criterion will help identify performance bottlenecks, allowing you to focus your optimization efforts on the most critical areas. Rust's low-level control over memory, combined with its high-level abstractions, makes it an ideal language for achieving optimal performance without sacrificing safety or expressiveness.

Chapter 10.

Advanced Topics and Future Directions

This section explores cutting-edge concepts in Rust and functional programming, offering a glimpse into advanced topics and the future of the language. As Rust continues to evolve, its integration with functional programming and its applications in various domains provide exciting opportunities for developers.

1. Advanced Functional Programming in Rust

Rust offers rich support for functional paradigms, including monads, functors, and applicatives, as well as advanced concepts like algebraic effects. These techniques allow developers to write more declarative, composable, and reusable code, pushing the boundaries of functional programming in a systems language.

2. Rust in Systems-Level Programming

Rust's guarantees of memory safety without a garbage collector make it ideal for systems programming, from operating systems to embedded systems. Developers are exploring how functional programming principles can improve the safety and readability of low-level code while maintaining performance.

3. Domain-Specific Languages (DSLs)

Rust's expressive type system and macros make it an excellent choice for creating DSLs. These custom languages are becoming increasingly common in areas like data processing, domain modeling, and embedded systems, enabling more domain-specific and functional designs.

4. Parallelism and Concurrency Innovations

Rust's ownership model eliminates many concurrency issues at compile time, but the language continues to evolve with frameworks like Tokio and Rayon for async programming and data-parallel computation. Future directions include enhancements in work-stealing algorithms and composable concurrency abstractions.

5. Category Theory and Mathematical Models

Rust's functional foundations open avenues for integrating category theory and mathematical models in software development. These advanced techniques can help developers design systems that are both rigorously correct and elegantly abstract.

6. Interfacing with Other Languages

Rust's ability to interoperate with languages like C, Python, and JavaScript is expanding its use in hybrid environments. Developers are exploring how functional programming paradigms in Rust can complement procedural and object-oriented paradigms in other ecosystems.

7. Rust in Emerging Domains

Rust is gaining traction in emerging fields such as blockchain, AI/ML, and quantum computing. Functional programming techniques in these areas can enhance the safety, efficiency, and scalability of new technologies.

8. The Future of Functional Programming in Rust

With growing community interest, Rust may see the development of new functional libraries and frameworks. Features like const generics, GATs (generic associated types), and type-level programming could further enrich functional programming capabilities in Rust.

Conclusion

Rust's fusion of functional and systems programming continues to redefine the possibilities for safe, efficient, and expressive code. By embracing advanced topics and staying attuned to future trends, developers can unlock the full potential of Rust in both traditional and emerging domains.

10.1 Category Theory and Functional Programming in Rust

Category theory is a branch of mathematics that provides a unifying framework for understanding abstract structures and their relationships. It has become an important foundation for functional programming, offering concepts such as functors, monads, and applicatives to model computations and data transformations. Rust, while not a purely functional language, supports many of these constructs, enabling developers to apply category theory principles in practical programming.

1. What is Category Theory?

At its core, category theory deals with objects and morphisms (arrows between objects) that satisfy specific compositional rules. Key principles include:

Composition: Morphisms can be composed to form new morphisms, and this composition must be associative.
Identity: Each object has an identity morphism that acts as a neutral element in composition.
These principles are abstract but directly applicable to programming constructs like functions, types, and transformations.

2. Category Theory in Functional Programming

Functional programming leverages category theory to structure computations and data manipulations. Some key abstractions include:

Functors: Represent mappings between categories, typically implemented as containers or structures (e.g., Option, Vec in Rust) that can be transformed while preserving their structure.

Monads: Extend functors by modeling sequential computations. They provide a way to chain operations, handling contexts like errors, optional values, or asynchronous computations.

Applicatives: Sit between functors and monads, enabling function application within a computational context.

3. Functors in Rust

In Rust, the Functor concept is often implemented using the map function for structures like Option or Result. A functor allows you to apply a function to a value inside a context without altering the context itself.

Example of Functor:

```rust
Copy code
let some_value = Some(5);
let result = some_value.map(|x| x + 1); // Transform value inside the context
assert_eq!(result, Some(6));
```

Here, map applies a function to the inner value of Some while preserving the Option context.

4. Monads in Rust

Monads provide a way to handle sequential computations with chaining. In Rust, monadic behavior is exhibited through methods like and_then (or flatMap in other languages), which allows chaining operations that produce monadic results.

Example of Monad:

rust
Copy code
```rust
fn divide(a: f64, b: f64) -> Option<f64> {
    if b != 0.0 {
        Some(a / b)
    } else {
        None
    }
}
```

```rust
let result = Some(10.0)
    .and_then(|x| divide(x, 2.0))
        .and_then(|x| divide(x, 0.0)); // Handles computation
failure gracefully
assert_eq!(result, None);
```

5. Applicatives in Rust

Applicatives allow applying functions wrapped in a context (e.g., Option) to values in the same context. While Rust does not have a direct Applicative trait, this pattern can be emulated with libraries like fp-core or custom implementations.

Example of Applicative:

rust
Copy code
```rust
let add = |x: i32, y: i32| x + y;
let a = Some(2);
let b = Some(3);
```

```rust
let result = a.and_then(|x| b.map(|y| add(x, y))); // Combining contexts
assert_eq!(result, Some(5));
```

6. Composition in Rust

Category theory emphasizes composition as a fundamental principle. In Rust, function composition can be expressed using closures and higher-order functions, often to build pipelines or transformations.

Example of Function Composition:

```rust
rust
Copy code
fn add_one(x: i32) -> i32 { x + 1 }
fn double(x: i32) -> i32 { x * 2 }

let composed = |x| double(add_one(x));
assert_eq!(composed(3), 8);
```

7. Practical Applications in Rust

Error Handling: Using monads like Result enables chaining error-prone operations while avoiding deeply nested code.

Asynchronous Programming: Rust's Future is a monadic construct, allowing the chaining of async computations.
Data Transformation Pipelines: Category theory concepts simplify designing modular and composable data processing pipelines.

DSLs and Abstractions: By leveraging algebraic data types (enums and structs), Rust can model complex workflows inspired by category theory.

8. Libraries Supporting Category Theory in Rust

fp-core.rs: A library for functional programming abstractions like functors, monads, and applicatives.

frunk: Provides generic functional programming constructs and tools.

cats-effect: Influences patterns for concurrency and effect management, adapted for Rust.

Conclusion

Category theory offers a robust mathematical foundation for functional programming, and Rust's features align well with these abstractions. By understanding and applying category-theoretic principles like functors, monads, and composition, developers can create safer, more expressive, and highly composable Rust programs. As the Rust ecosystem grows, further exploration of category theory is likely to bring even more powerful functional paradigms to the language.

10.2 Functional Programming for Embedded Systems

Embedded systems development involves working with resource-constrained environments where performance, reliability, and safety are paramount. While traditionally dominated by procedural and imperative programming styles, functional programming is gaining traction due to its emphasis on immutability, composability, and declarative design principles. Rust, with its blend of low-level control and functional programming features, is uniquely positioned to address the challenges of embedded systems.

1. Why Use Functional Programming in Embedded Systems?

Functional programming introduces paradigms that are particularly beneficial in the context of embedded systems:

Immutability: By avoiding mutable state, functional programming reduces side effects, which are a common source of bugs in concurrent or interrupt-driven systems.

Composability: Modular, reusable functions make it easier to design complex systems with predictable behavior.

Declarative Logic: Code that describes what to do rather than how to do it improves readability and maintainability.

Concurrency: Functional paradigms, such as immutability, simplify the design of concurrent and real-time systems, ensuring safe interaction with multiple threads or interrupts.

2. Rust's Functional Features in Embedded Systems

Rust provides several features that make functional programming feasible for embedded systems:

Ownership and Borrowing: Guarantees memory safety without a garbage collector, crucial for embedded environments.

Zero-Cost Abstractions: Functional constructs like iterators, closures, and pattern matching compile down to efficient, low-level code.

Static Typing and Compile-Time Checks: Rust ensures correctness at compile time, which is critical for systems where runtime failures can be catastrophic.

Concurrency Primitives: Rust's ownership model eliminates data races, enabling safer concurrent programming.

3. Functional Design Patterns in Embedded Systems

3.1 Pure Functions for Deterministic Behavior

Pure functions, which avoid side effects and depend solely on their inputs, are ideal for embedded systems. They ensure deterministic behavior, a critical requirement for real-time tasks.

Example:

rust

Copy code

```rust
fn calculate_pwm_duty_cycle(speed: u32, max_speed: u32) -> u8 {
    ((speed as f32 / max_speed as f32) * 255.0) as u8
}
```

3.2 Event Handling with Pattern Matching

Pattern matching simplifies event-driven programming by making the code more declarative and reducing branching logic.

Example:

rust

Copy code

```rust
enum Event {
    ButtonPressed,
    SensorTriggered(u16),
    Timeout,
}
```

```rust
fn handle_event(event: Event) {
    match event {
        Event::ButtonPressed => println!("Button was pressed!"),
        Event::SensorTriggered(value) => println!("Sensor triggered with value: {}", value),
        Event::Timeout => println!("Timeout occurred."),
    }
}
```

3.3 Immutable State Management

Immutable data structures, combined with functional update patterns, can help manage system state more predictably.

Example:

```rust
Copy code
struct SystemState {
    temperature: f32,
    humidity: f32,
```

```
}
```

```rust
fn update_temperature(state: &SystemState, new_temp:
f32) -> SystemState {
    SystemState {
        temperature: new_temp,
        ..*state
    }
}
```

3.4 Lazy Evaluation for Resource Efficiency

In embedded systems, lazy evaluation can defer computations until they are actually needed, optimizing resource usage. Rust's iterator trait enables lazy evaluation natively.

Example:

rust
Copy code
```rust
let data = [1, 2, 3, 4];
let squared: Vec<_> = data.iter()
```

```
.filter(|&&x| x % 2 == 0)
.map(|&x| x * x)
.collect();
```

4. Use Cases of Functional Programming in Embedded Systems

4.1 Signal Processing

Functional pipelines allow for elegant and efficient transformation of signals or sensor data, often used in IoT devices.

4.2 State Machines

Embedded systems often rely on state machines. Functional programming provides a clean way to define and transition between states using enums and pattern matching.

4.3 Concurrency in Real-Time Systems

With Rust's functional concurrency tools, it is possible to safely handle multiple tasks like sensor monitoring, communication, and control without worrying about race conditions or deadlocks.

4.4 Protocol Parsing

Immutable and composable data transformations are ideal for implementing lightweight parsers for communication protocols.

5. Challenges and Considerations

While functional programming offers many benefits for embedded systems, there are challenges to consider:

Learning Curve: Functional paradigms may be unfamiliar to embedded developers with a procedural background.

Performance Tuning: Care must be taken to avoid performance pitfalls like excessive allocation or recursion in resource-constrained environments.

Debugging: Higher abstraction levels can sometimes make debugging harder compared to lower-level imperative code.

6. Tools and Frameworks for Functional Embedded Rust

embedded-hal: A hardware abstraction layer for embedded Rust, enabling composable and reusable drivers.

async-embedded: Provides asynchronous primitives for embedded systems, leveraging functional programming paradigms.

heapless: Enables functional-style programming with fixed-capacity data structures for memory-constrained devices.

7. Conclusion

Functional programming brings a fresh perspective to embedded systems development, focusing on safety, composability, and correctness. With Rust's strong functional programming capabilities and system-level performance, developers can harness the best of both worlds to create reliable and efficient embedded solutions.

10.3 Exploring the Rust Functional Ecosystem: Libraries and Tools

Rust's growing ecosystem supports a wide range of functional programming paradigms, enabling developers to write expressive, concise, and efficient code. These libraries and tools provide abstractions for functional patterns, error handling, concurrency, and more, helping developers implement functional programming techniques in various domains.

1. Functional Programming Libraries in Rust

1.1 fp-core.rs

A lightweight library for functional programming in Rust. It introduces abstractions like functors, applicatives, and monads, making it easier to compose functions and handle complex transformations.

Key Features:

Implements functional constructs like map, flat_map, and zip.
Provides tools for working with effects and functional composition.

Example Usage:

```rust
Copy code
use fp_core::prelude::*;
let result = Some(5).map(|x| x + 1).map(|x| x * 2);
assert_eq!(result, Some(12));
```

1.2 frunk

A functional programming toolkit for generic programming in Rust. It emphasizes immutability, functional transformations, and compile-time safety.

Key Features:

Generic data types and higher-order functions.
Functional transformations on data structures.
HList (heterogeneous list) for type-safe programming.

Example Usage:

```rust
Copy code
use frunk::hlist;
let list = hlist![1, "hello", 3.14];
```

1.3 itertools

Extends Rust's standard library iterators with additional methods, making it easier to write functional-style transformations and data pipelines.

Key Features:

Methods for folding, grouping, zipping, and more.
Lazy evaluation for efficient processing.

Example Usage:

```rust
Copy code
use itertools::Itertools;
let nums = vec![1, 2, 3, 4];
let sum = nums.iter().filter(|&&x| x % 2 == 0).map(|&x| x * 2).sum::<i32>();
assert_eq!(sum, 12);
```

1.4 functional-rs

A functional programming library that introduces common abstractions like OptionT, ResultT, and combinators for chaining operations.

Key Features:

Transformational combinators for Option and Result. Simplifies chaining and composition of operations.

2. Libraries for Functional Concurrency

2.1 rayon

Rayon simplifies parallel processing with a functional interface, enabling concurrent computations while abstracting away threading complexity.

Key Features:

Parallel iterators for data-intensive tasks.
Functional methods like map, filter, and reduce.

Example Usage:

```rust
Copy code
use rayon::prelude::*;
let nums: Vec<i32> = (1..10).collect();
let sum: i32 = nums.par_iter().map(|x| x * 2).sum();
```

```
assert_eq!(sum, 90);
```

2.2 async-std and tokio

Both libraries provide tools for asynchronous programming. They support chaining operations on futures, a functional approach to managing async workflows.

Key Features:

Stream-based processing for async data.
Functional-style combinators for managing concurrency.

Example Usage:

```rust
Copy code
use async_std::task;

async fn fetch_data() -> String {
    "data".to_string()
}
```

```rust
let data = task::block_on(fetch_data());
```

3. Data Transformation and Functional Utilities

3.1 serde

While primarily a serialization/deserialization library, serde works well in functional pipelines for transforming structured data.

Key Features:

Composable data serialization.
Functional-style transformations on data structures.
.

Example Usage:

```rust
rust
Copy code
use serde_json::json;
let data = json!({"key": "value"});
```
3.2 nalgebra and ndarray

For scientific computing and data processing, these libraries enable functional-style matrix and array operations.

Key Features:

Functional operations on arrays and matrices.
Lazy evaluation for large datasets.

Example Usage:

```rust
Copy code
use ndarray::Array;
let arr = Array::from_vec(vec![1, 2, 3, 4]).map(|x| x * 2);
```

4. Exploring Functional Patterns in Domain-Specific Libraries

4.1 diesel

A functional-style ORM that uses Rust's type system to compose safe and efficient database queries.

Key Features:

Composable queries.

Type-safe SQL-like syntax.

Example Usage:

rust
Copy code
```
use diesel::prelude::*;
let                          results                        =
users.filter(age.gt(18)).load::<User>(&connection)?;
```

4.2 nom

A parser combinator library for building parsers in a functional style.

Key Features:

Composable parser primitives.

Zero-copy parsing for performance.

Example Usage:

```rust
Copy code
use nom::character::complete::digit1;
let parser = digit1;
assert_eq!(parser("123"), Ok(("", "123")));
```

5. Tools for Functional Testing

5.1 quickcheck

A property-based testing framework inspired by Haskell's QuickCheck. It automatically generates test cases based on properties of your functions.

Key Features:

Automates test case generation.

Functional-style validation of invariants.

Example Usage:

rust
Copy code
```
#[quickcheck]
fn test_addition(a: i32, b: i32) -> bool {
    a + b == b + a
}
```

6. IDEs and Editors Supporting Functional Rust

rust-analyzer: Provides code completion and linting, supporting functional constructs in Rust.
cargo-expand: Expands macros to show the generated code, useful for understanding functional-style abstractions.

Conclusion

The Rust ecosystem offers powerful libraries and tools for adopting functional programming principles in various applications. From foundational utilities like itertools to domain-specific tools like nom and diesel, these resources make it easier to write expressive, efficient, and composable Rust code. By leveraging these tools, developers can harness the full potential of Rust's functional programming capabilities.

10.4 Combining Functional and Imperative Styles

Rust is a multi-paradigm programming language that excels at blending functional and imperative programming styles. This combination allows developers to leverage the expressive, declarative power of functional programming while maintaining the performance and control provided by imperative programming. Understanding how and when to combine these styles can lead to more effective, readable, and efficient code.

1. The Case for Combining Styles

Each programming style has strengths that suit different use cases:

Functional Programming: Emphasizes immutability, composability, and declarative problem-solving. It shines in tasks like data transformation, concurrency, and error handling.
Imperative Programming: Focuses on explicit control flow and mutable state, making it ideal for low-level operations, system programming, and performance-critical sections.

By combining these paradigms, developers can:

Write high-level, expressive code for business logic.
Use low-level, imperative constructs for performance-critical tasks.
Create modular, maintainable, and efficient programs.

2. Functional Constructs in an Imperative Context

Rust allows you to introduce functional concepts in imperative workflows, making code more concise and expressive.

2.1 Using Iterators and Closures

Iterators and closures bring functional abstractions to loops, reducing boilerplate while preserving control over flow.

Example:

```rust
Copy code
let nums = vec![1, 2, 3, 4, 5];
let doubled: Vec<_> = nums.iter().map(|x| x * 2).collect();
println!("{:?}", doubled); // Output: [2, 4, 6, 8, 10]
```

2.2 Pattern Matching in Control Flow

Pattern matching provides a declarative way to handle control flow, replacing traditional conditional logic.

Example:

rust

Copy code

```rust
let status_code = 200;
match status_code {
    200 => println!("OK"),
    404 => println!("Not Found"),
    _ => println!("Unknown Status"),
}
```

2.3 Functional Error Handling in Imperative Code

Rust's Result and Option types introduce functional error handling while preserving imperative readability.

Example:

rust

Copy code

```rust
fn divide(a: i32, b: i32) -> Option<i32> {
    if b != 0 {
        Some(a / b)
    } else {
```

```
        None
    }
}

let result = divide(10, 2).unwrap_or_else(|| {
    println!("Cannot divide by zero");
    0
});
println!("{}", result); // Output: 5
```

3. Introducing Imperative Constructs in Functional Code

While functional programming encourages immutability, some scenarios demand imperative constructs for performance or simplicity.

3.1 Mutable State with Functional Encapsulation

You can use mutable state within functions while ensuring it doesn't leak out.

Example:

rust

Copy code

```rust
fn sum_of_squares(nums: &[i32]) -> i32 {
    let mut sum = 0;
    for &num in nums {
        sum += num * num;
    }
    sum
}
```

3.2 Early Exits in Functional Code

Imperative constructs like break and return can simplify logic within functional transformations.

Example:

rust

Copy code

```rust
let nums = vec![1, 2, 3, 4, 5];
for &num in &nums {
    if num > 3 {
```

```
        println!("Found: {}", num);
        break;
    }
}
```

4. Best Practices for Blending Styles

4.1 Prioritize Readability

Choose the style that makes the code more understandable for the given context. Use functional pipelines for transformations and imperative constructs for explicit control.

4.2 Use Functional Constructs for High-Level Logic

Apply functional techniques for operations like filtering, mapping, and folding, where the logic is declarative.

4.3 Optimize Performance-Critical Sections Imperatively

When dealing with performance bottlenecks, such as in embedded or real-time systems, leverage Rust's low-level imperative features.

4.4 Isolate Styles for Clarity

Encapsulate functional and imperative logic in separate functions or modules to maintain code clarity.

5. Example: Combining Both Styles

Here's an example that combines functional transformations and imperative control:

Example:

rust
Copy code
```rust
fn process_numbers(nums: Vec<i32>) -> Vec<i32> {
    nums.into_iter()
        .filter(|&x| x % 2 == 0) // Functional filtering
        .map(|x| {
            let mut result = x * 2; // Imperative modification
```

```rust
        if result > 10 {
            result = 10;
        }
        result
    })
    .collect()
}

fn main() {
    let nums = vec![1, 2, 3, 4, 5, 6];
    let processed = process_numbers(nums);
    println!("{:?}", processed); // Output: [4, 8, 10]
}
```

6. Advantages of Combining Styles

Flexibility: Choose the best paradigm for each part of your application.

Performance: Write high-level logic while retaining low-level control when needed.

Expressiveness: Create more concise and readable code using functional abstractions.

Maintainability: Encapsulate imperative code in functional interfaces for better modularity.

Conclusion

Rust empowers developers to blend functional and imperative styles seamlessly, enabling them to write expressive, efficient, and maintainable code. By understanding the strengths of each paradigm and how to combine them effectively, developers can build robust solutions that leverage the best of both worlds.

Chapter 11

. Best Practices for Functional Rust

Functional programming in Rust enables expressive, concise, and safe code. To make the most of this paradigm, it's essential to follow best practices that align with Rust's design philosophy.

1. Embrace Immutability

Prefer immutable variables (let) over mutable ones (let mut) to reduce unintended side effects.
Use immutability to make functions more predictable and thread-safe.

Example:

rust
Copy code

```rust
let numbers = vec![1, 2, 3];
let doubled: Vec<_> = numbers.iter().map(|x| x * 2).collect();
```

2. Use Pure Functions

Write functions without side effects, ensuring they depend only on their inputs and produce consistent outputs.
Pure functions improve testability and composability.

Example:

rust
Copy code
```rust
fn square(x: i32) -> i32 {
    x * x
}
```

3. Leverage Iterators and Functional Pipelines

Replace explicit loops with iterators and methods like map, filter, and fold.

Use chaining to create concise and expressive pipelines.

Example:

rust

Copy code

```
let sum: i32 = (1..10).filter(|x| x % 2 == 0).sum();
```

4. Favor Pattern Matching

Use match and if let to handle enums (Option, Result) effectively.
Pattern matching improves readability and eliminates boilerplate error handling.

Example:

rust

Copy code

```
match some_value {
    Some(val) => println!("Value: {}", val),
    None => println!("No value"),
}
```

5. Use Combinators for Error Handling

Replace verbose error handling with combinators like map, and_then, and unwrap_or_else.

Example:

rust
Copy code
```
let result = some_result.map(|x| x * 2).unwrap_or(0);
```

6. Compose Small, Reusable Functions

Break down complex logic into smaller, composable functions.
Use higher-order functions to abstract repetitive patterns.

Example:

rust
Copy code

```rust
fn add(x: i32) -> i32 {
    x + 1
}

fn double(x: i32) -> i32 {
    x * 2
}

let result = add(double(5)); // 11
```

7. Optimize with Lazy Evaluation

Use lazy evaluation (e.g., iterators) for performance, especially when working with large datasets or infinite sequences.

Example:

rust
Copy code
```rust
let result: Vec<_> = (1..).take(10).map(|x| x * 2).collect();
```

8. Combine Functional and Imperative Styles

Use functional abstractions for high-level logic and imperative constructs for performance-critical sections. Blend paradigms to write expressive and efficient code.

9. Avoid Overuse of Functional Abstractions

Rust prioritizes practicality over strict functional purity. Avoid overly complex abstractions that hinder readability or performance.

10. Write Tests for Functional Logic

Use property-based testing (e.g., with quickcheck) to validate functional code.
Test edge cases to ensure robustness of functional pipelines.

Example:

rust
Copy code
```
#[quickcheck]
```

```rust
fn test_addition(a: i32, b: i32) -> bool {
    add(a, b) == add(b, a)
}
```

Conclusion

By following these best practices, you can write functional Rust code that is safe, efficient, and easy to maintain. Balancing functional principles with Rust's unique features ensures robust and high-performing applications.

11.1 Writing Idiomatic Functional Rust Code

Writing idiomatic functional Rust code involves adhering to the language's principles while leveraging functional programming techniques. By following Rust's

415

conventions and embracing its features, developers can produce expressive, safe, and efficient code that aligns with community standards.

1. Use Immutability and Pure Functions

Favor immutable variables (let) to avoid unintended side effects.
Write pure functions that rely only on inputs and produce predictable outputs.

Example:

rust
Copy code
```rust
fn square(x: i32) -> i32 {
    x * x
}
```

```rust
let result = square(4); // 16
```

2. Favor Functional Iterators Over Loops

Replace imperative loops with iterators and functional combinators like map, filter, and fold.

Avoid manual indexing where iterators suffice.

Example:

rust
Copy code
```
let nums = vec![1, 2, 3, 4];
let doubled: Vec<_> = nums.iter().map(|x| x * 2).collect();
```

3. Use Pattern Matching for Control Flow

Leverage pattern matching (match and if let) for concise and expressive control flow, especially with enums like Option and Result.

Example:

rust
Copy code
```
fn divide(a: i32, b: i32) -> Option<i32> {
    if b != 0 {
```

```rust
        Some(a / b)
    } else {
        None
    }
}


match divide(10, 2) {
    Some(result) => println!("Result: {}", result),
    None => println!("Cannot divide by zero"),
}
```

4. Compose Functions for Readability

Break complex operations into smaller, reusable functions and compose them to achieve clarity and modularity.

Example:

rust
Copy code
```rust
fn add_one(x: i32) -> i32 {
    x + 1
```

```
}

fn double(x: i32) -> i32 {
    x * 2
}

fn process(num: i32) -> i32 {
    double(add_one(num))
}

let result = process(3); // 8
```

5. Leverage Closures for Inline Logic

Use closures for compact and flexible inline functionality, especially in iterator pipelines.

Example:

rust
Copy code
```
let nums = vec![1, 2, 3];
let squares: Vec<_> = nums.iter().map(|x| x * x).collect();
```

6. Adopt Functional Error Handling

Use combinators like map, and_then, unwrap_or, and unwrap_or_else for concise error handling with Option and Result.

Example:

```rust
Copy code
let input = Some(5);
let doubled = input.map(|x| x * 2).unwrap_or(0);
println!("{}", doubled); // 10
```

7. Embrace Enum-Based Design

Use enums to represent state and ensure exhaustive handling with pattern matching.
Avoid using magic values like -1 or None to indicate state.

Example:

```rust
Copy code
enum Status {
    Success,
    Failure(String),
}

fn handle_status(status: Status) {
    match status {
        Status::Success => println!("Operation successful"),
        Status::Failure(err) => println!("Error: {}", err),
    }
}
```

8. Utilize Algebraic Data Types

Combine structs and enums for modeling complex data in a functional style.

Example:

```rust
Copy code
enum Shape {
    Circle { radius: f64 },
    Rectangle { width: f64, height: f64 },
}

fn area(shape: Shape) -> f64 {
    match shape {
        Shape::Circle { radius } => 3.14 * radius * radius,
        Shape::Rectangle { width, height } => width * height,
    }
}
```

9. Prioritize Lazy Evaluation with Iterators

Use lazy evaluation to optimize performance, especially for large or infinite datasets.

Example:

```rust
Copy code
```

```
let sum: i32 = (1..).take(10).filter(|x| x % 2 == 0).sum();
```

10. Write Idiomatic Error Messages

Use Result with descriptive error types and messages to clearly convey issues.
Implement the From or Into traits for custom error conversion.

Example:

rust
Copy code
```
fn parse_number(input: &str) -> Result<i32, String> {
        input.parse::<i32>().map_err(|_|    "Invalid
number".to_string())
}
```

11. Prefer Declarative Over Imperative Logic

Strive for declarative expressions that describe what to do rather than how to do it.

Example:

Imperative:

rust
Copy code
```rust
let mut evens = vec![];
for i in 1..10 {
    if i % 2 == 0 {
        evens.push(i);
    }
}
```

Declarative:

rust
Copy code
```rust
let evens: Vec<_> = (1..10).filter(|x| x % 2 == 0).collect();
```

12. Optimize for Zero-Cost Abstractions

Use Rust's features like iterators and traits to write high-level code without sacrificing performance.

Conclusion

Idiomatic functional Rust combines the expressiveness of functional programming with the performance and safety guarantees of Rust. By following these practices, developers can write concise, modular, and maintainable code that adheres to Rust's philosophy and community standards.

11.2 Testing Functional Programs in Rust

Testing is a critical aspect of software development, and Rust's robust testing framework makes it particularly effective for functional programming. Functional programs are often easier to test due to their reliance on pure functions, immutability, and composability. This ensures predictable behavior and facilitates thorough validation of logic.

1. Writing Unit Tests for Pure Functions

Pure functions are deterministic and have no side effects, making them ideal candidates for unit testing.

Example:

```rust
Copy code
fn add(a: i32, b: i32) -> i32 {
    a + b
}

#[cfg(test)]
mod tests {
    use super::*;

    #[test]
    fn test_add() {
        assert_eq!(add(2, 3), 5);
    }
}
```

Best Practice: Write tests for edge cases to ensure function robustness.

2. Testing Higher-Order Functions

Functional programs often use higher-order functions, which can be tested by supplying different closures as inputs.

Example:

```rust
Copy code
fn apply_twice<F>(x: i32, f: F) -> i32
where
    F: Fn(i32) -> i32,
{
    f(f(x))
}

#[cfg(test)]
mod tests {
    use super::*;
```

```
    #[test]
    fn test_apply_twice() {
        let result = apply_twice(2, |x| x + 1);
        assert_eq!(result, 4);
    }
}
```

3. Property-Based Testing

Rust supports property-based testing via crates like quickcheck and proptest. These frameworks test functions with automatically generated input data to validate properties of the logic.

Example:

rust
Copy code
```
use quickcheck::quickcheck;

fn add_is_commutative(a: i32, b: i32) -> bool {
    add(a, b) == add(b, a)
```

```
}
```

```
quickcheck! {
    fn test_add_is_commutative(a: i32, b: i32) -> bool {
        add_is_commutative(a, b)
    }
}
```

Benefit: Catches edge cases that may not be covered by traditional unit tests.

4. Testing Functional Pipelines

When testing functional pipelines built with iterators or combinators, verify both the intermediate states and final output.

Example:

rust
Copy code
```
fn double_evens(numbers: Vec<i32>) -> Vec<i32> {
    numbers.into_iter().filter(|x| x % 2 == 0).map(|x| x *
2).collect()
```

```
}

#[cfg(test)]
mod tests {
    use super::*;

    #[test]
    fn test_double_evens() {
        let input = vec![1, 2, 3, 4];
        let expected = vec![4, 8];
        assert_eq!(double_evens(input), expected);
    }
}
```

5. Testing Enums and Pattern Matching

Functional design often involves enums and pattern matching. Ensure all possible cases are covered in your tests.

Example:

rust

```
Copy code
enum Status {
    Success,
    Failure(String),
}

fn process(status: Status) -> String {
    match status {
        Status::Success => "All good".to_string(),
        Status::Failure(reason) => format!("Error: {}", reason),
    }
}

#[cfg(test)]
mod tests {
    use super::*;

    #[test]
    fn test_process() {
        assert_eq!(process(Status::Success), "All good");
        assert_eq!(process(Status::Failure("Network
issue".to_string())), "Error: Network issue");
    }
```

```
}
```

6. Mocking and Dependency Injection

For functions that interact with external dependencies, use traits and mock implementations to isolate functional logic in tests.

Example:

```rust
Copy code
trait DataFetcher {
    fn fetch_data(&self) -> Vec<i32>;
}

struct MockFetcher;

impl DataFetcher for MockFetcher {
    fn fetch_data(&self) -> Vec<i32> {
        vec![1, 2, 3]
    }
}
```

```rust
fn process_data<F: DataFetcher>(fetcher: F) -> Vec<i32> {
    fetcher.fetch_data().into_iter().map(|x| x * 2).collect()
}

#[cfg(test)]
mod tests {
    use super::*;

    #[test]
    fn test_process_data() {
        let mock_fetcher = MockFetcher;
        assert_eq!(process_data(mock_fetcher), vec![2, 4, 6]);
    }
}
```

7. Benchmarking Functional Programs

Functional abstractions can sometimes introduce performance trade-offs. Use Rust's benchmarking tools (cargo bench) or external crates like criterion to profile and optimize functional code.

Example:

```rust
Copy code
#[bench]
fn bench_double_evens(b: &mut Bencher) {
    let input = (1..1000).collect::<Vec<_>>();
    b.iter(|| double_evens(input.clone()));
}
```

8. Debugging Functional Code

Use .inspect() with iterators to log intermediate states during testing.
Leverage dbg!() to print debug information without interrupting functional pipelines.

Example:

```rust
Copy code
let result: Vec<_> = (1..5)
    .inspect(|x| dbg!(x))
```

```
.map(|x| x * 2)
.collect();
```

Conclusion

Testing functional programs in Rust is streamlined by the language's safety features, functional combinators, and testing ecosystem. Whether you're writing unit tests, property-based tests, or benchmarking pipelines, Rust's tools and techniques empower developers to validate functional logic thoroughly and efficiently.

11.3 Debugging and Troubleshooting Functional Rust

Debugging functional Rust programs involves understanding the functional paradigm and leveraging Rust's powerful debugging tools. Functional programs often rely on immutability, pure functions, and compositional pipelines, which can simplify reasoning about code but introduce unique challenges in identifying issues. Here's how to approach debugging functional Rust effectively:

1. Leverage Compiler Messages

Rust's compiler provides detailed and actionable error messages, especially when dealing with type mismatches, ownership issues, or borrow checker violations.

Read errors carefully: Rust often suggests fixes or points to the exact location of the issue.
Use the --verbose flag with cargo commands for additional context.

Example:

```bash
Copy code
error[E0382]: borrow of moved value: `x`
 --> main.rs:5:13
```

```
  |
4 | let x = String::from("hello");
  |    - value moved here
5 | println!("{}", x);
  |          ^ value borrowed here after move
```

2. Use dbg! for Debugging Pipelines

The dbg! macro allows you to print intermediate values during the execution of functional pipelines. It outputs both the variable and its value.

Example:

rust
Copy code
```rust
let result: Vec<_> = (1..5)
    .map(|x| dbg!(x * 2)) // Debug intermediate computation
    .collect();
```

3. Debug with .inspect() in Iterators

The .inspect() method in iterator pipelines lets you log intermediate values without modifying the logic.

Example:

rust
Copy code
```
let result: Vec<_> = (1..5)
    .map(|x| x * 2)
    .inspect(|x| println!("Value: {}", x)) // Log each value
    .collect();
```

4. Use Rust's Logging Framework

Add the log and env_logger crates to your project for structured debugging output.
Replace println! with structured log messages for better debugging in larger applications.

Example:

rust
Copy code

```rust
use log::info;

fn process_data(data: Vec<i32>) -> Vec<i32> {
    data.into_iter()
        .map(|x| {
            info!("Processing value: {}", x);
            x * 2
        })
        .collect()
}

fn main() {
    env_logger::init();
    let data = vec![1, 2, 3];
    let result = process_data(data);
}
```

5. Debugging Closures and Higher-Order Functions

When closures fail to compile or behave unexpectedly, ensure you understand:

Captured environment: Closures automatically capture variables from their surrounding scope.

Trait bounds: Verify that the closure satisfies required traits (e.g., Fn, FnMut, FnOnce).

Common Error:

bash
Copy code
error[E0277]: a closure cannot be invoked twice if it moves its captured variables

Fix: Use a closure that borrows instead of moves, or adjust the closure type in the function signature.

6. Handle Option and Result Effectively

Use combinators like map, and_then, and unwrap_or_else for concise error handling.

Log errors or fallback values to identify edge cases during runtime.

Example:

rust

Copy code

```
let input: Option<i32> = Some(10);
let doubled = input
    .map(|x| x * 2)
    .unwrap_or_else(|| {
        println!("Input was None, using default value");
        0
    });
```

7. Diagnose Pattern Matching Issues

Pattern matching is central to functional Rust but can be error-prone if patterns are incomplete or too generic.

Use exhaustive matching to ensure all cases are handled. Log unmatched patterns with _ to detect unexpected inputs.

Example:

rust

Copy code

```
match value {
    Some(x) if x > 0 => println!("Positive value: {}", x),
    Some(x) => println!("Non-positive value: {}", x),
    None => println!("No value provided"),
    _ => println!("Unexpected case"), // Catch-all for debugging
}
```

8. Understand Borrow Checker Errors

The borrow checker is a frequent source of issues when working with closures or iterators in Rust.

Tip: Break pipelines into smaller steps to identify where ownership conflicts arise.
Use .cloned() or .to_owned() to resolve borrowing issues, but only when appropriate.

9. Utilize Rust Backtraces

When a program panics, enable backtraces to identify the source of the issue.

Run your program with the RUST_BACKTRACE=1
environment variable.

Example:

bash
Copy code
RUST_BACKTRACE=1 cargo run

10. Debugging with Tools

Rust provides several tools for advanced debugging:

GDB or LLDB: Use these debuggers for low-level
insights into compiled Rust binaries.
VSCode Debugger: Integrate Rust debugging into your
IDE for a graphical interface.
Cargo Expand: Inspect macros and generated code to
debug complex constructs.

bash
Copy code

```
cargo install cargo-expand
cargo expand
```

11. Benchmark and Profile Functional Pipelines

Functional pipelines can introduce performance bottlenecks if not optimized. Use profiling tools like perf or the criterion crate to pinpoint slow operations.

Example:

```rust
Copy code
#[bench]
fn bench_pipeline(b: &mut Bencher) {
    let data = (1..1_000).collect::<Vec<_>>();
    b.iter(|| data.iter().map(|x| x * 2).collect::<Vec<_>>());
}
```

12. Common Debugging Pitfalls in Functional Rust

Iterator Lifetimes: Ensure iterators do not outlive the data they reference.

Closure Capture: Be aware of closures that move instead of borrow variables.

Infinite Iterators: Avoid creating infinite loops by forgetting a .take() or similar limiter.

Conclusion

Debugging functional Rust programs is greatly simplified by Rust's powerful tooling, strict compiler checks, and predictable functional patterns. By combining these techniques with thoughtful design, developers can efficiently diagnose and resolve issues while maintaining the clarity and safety of their functional code.

11.4 Ensuring Code Readability and Maintainability

Readable and maintainable code is essential for long-term success in software development. In Rust, leveraging its functional programming capabilities and idiomatic practices ensures code is not only efficient but also easy to understand, extend, and debug. Here's how to achieve this:

1. Embrace Idiomatic Rust

Rust's community emphasizes idiomatic practices, which promote consistency and clarity. Follow these principles:

Use snake_case for variable and function names.
Prefer let bindings over mutable variables unless mutation is necessary.
Use ? for error propagation instead of manual match handling.

Example:

rust
Copy code
```rust
fn process_file(path: &str) -> Result<String, std::io::Error> {
```

```
    let content = std::fs::read_to_string(path)?;
    Ok(content)
}
```

2. Modularize Code with Functions and Modules

Break Down Complex Logic: Decompose large functions into smaller, reusable pieces with descriptive names. Organize related functionality in modules and use mod.rs for grouping.

Example:

```rust
Copy code
// src/math.rs
pub fn add(a: i32, b: i32) -> i32 {
    a + b
}

// src/main.rs
mod math;
```

```
fn main() {
    let result = math::add(2, 3);
    println!("Result: {}", result);
}
```

3. Favor Functional Abstractions for Clarity

Functional programming techniques like iterators, combinators, and closures reduce boilerplate and make the intent clear.

Avoid explicit loops when higher-order methods like .map() or .filter() suffice.

Example:

rust
Copy code
```
let evens: Vec<_> = (1..10).filter(|x| x % 2 == 0).collect();
```

4. Use Descriptive Names and Comments

Variable and Function Names: Names should describe their purpose and avoid abbreviations.

Comments: Explain non-obvious logic or domain-specific knowledge, but avoid over-commenting trivial code.

Example:

rust
Copy code
```rust
/// Calculates the factorial of a number.
/// Uses recursion for simplicity.
fn factorial(n: u32) -> u32 {
    match n {
        0 => 1,
        _ => n * factorial(n - 1),
    }
}
```

5. Leverage Pattern Matching for Readability

Pattern matching makes code easier to read and avoids nested conditionals.

Example:

rust
Copy code
```rust
fn describe_number(n: i32) -> &'static str {
    match n {
        0 => "Zero",
        1..=10 => "Small number",
        _ => "Large number",
    }
}
```

6. Ensure Comprehensive Error Handling

Use Rust's Result and Option types to handle errors gracefully.
Employ combinators like map, and_then, or unwrap_or_else for concise error propagation.

Example:

rust

```
Copy code
fn get_length(input: Option<&str>) -> usize {
    input.map_or(0, |s| s.len())
}
```

7. Document with rustdoc

Rust's built-in documentation tool, rustdoc, generates API documentation from comments.

Use /// for public items and //! for module-level documentation.

Example:

rust
Copy code
```
/// Adds two numbers.
///
/// # Examples
/// ```
/// let result = add(2, 3);
/// assert_eq!(result, 5);
```

```
/// ```
pub fn add(a: i32, b: i32) -> i32 {
    a + b
}
```

8. Avoid Overengineering

Use simple solutions that fulfill current requirements without unnecessary abstraction.
Avoid adding functional layers or types unless they enhance clarity or functionality.

Bad Example (Overengineered):

```rust
Copy code
fn add<F>(a: i32, b: i32, f: F) -> i32
where
    F: Fn(i32, i32) -> i32,
{
    f(a, b)
}
```

add(2, 3, |x, y| x + y);

Better:

rust
Copy code
```rust
fn add(a: i32, b: i32) -> i32 {
    a + b
}
```

9. Maintain a Consistent Style

Use tools like rustfmt to enforce consistent formatting. Run clippy to identify potential bugs or non-idiomatic constructs.

Command to Format Code:

bash
Copy code
```bash
cargo fmt
```

Command to Run Clippy:

```bash
Copy code
cargo clippy
```

10. Test and Refactor Regularly

Write tests for every new feature or bug fix to prevent regressions.
Refactor code regularly to remove duplication, improve readability, and enhance performance.

Example:

```rust
Copy code
#[cfg(test)]
mod tests {
    use super::*;

    #[test]
    fn test_add() {
        assert_eq!(add(2, 3), 5);
    }
```

```
}
```

11. Use Type Aliases and Newtypes

Use type aliases or newtypes to clarify intent and improve readability.

Example:

rust
Copy code
```rust
type Kilometers = u32;

fn calculate_distance(distance: Kilometers) -> Kilometers
{
    distance * 2
}
```

Conclusion

By adopting idiomatic Rust practices, leveraging functional abstractions, and using tooling effectively, you can create Rust programs that are both readable and maintainable. These strategies not only improve collaboration and debugging but also make the codebase adapt

www.ingramcontent.com/pod-product-compliance
Lightning Source LLC
LaVergne TN
LVHW022332060326
832902LV00022B/4002